IN HIGH PLACES

WITH

HENRY DAVID THOREAU

IN HIGH PLACES

WITH

HENRY DAVID THOREAU

A Hiker's Guide with Routes & Maps

John Gibson

COUNTRYMAN PRESS
Woodstock, Vermont

Remembering
Bessie Hanson Gibson
and
John Edward Gibson

Quotations from the works of Henry David Thoreau, including *Correspondence*, *Journals*, *The Maine Woods*, *Walden*, and *A Week on the Concord and Merrimack Rivers* are from the digitized collections of the Thoreau Institute of the Walden Woods Project. Additional Thoreau quotations are from *The Maine Woods* (2009), edited and annotated by Jeffrey S. Cramer; from *Wild Fruits* (2000), edited and introduced by Bradley P. Dean; and from *The Journal of Henry David Thoreau, 1837–1861* (2009), edited by Damion Searles.

Interior photographs by the author unless otherwise specified
Book design and composition by Eugenie S. Delaney

Published by The Countryman Press, P.O. Box 748, Woodstock, VT 05091

Distributed by W. W. Norton & Company, Inc., 500 Fifth Avenue, New York, NY 10110

Printed in the United States of America

10 9 8 7 6 5 4 3 2 1

In High Places with Henry David Thoreau
978-1-58157-196-7

Contents

———◦◉◦———

Introduction

—⊶◈⊷—

It is only when we forget all our learning that
we begin to know. I do not get nearer by a
hair's breadth to any natural object so long as
I presume that I have an introduction to it
from some learned man. . . . If you would
make acquaintance with ferns you must forget
your botany.

—*JOURNAL*, OCTOBER 4, 1859

I n September of 1851, Henry David Thoreau wrote,
"The scenery, when it is truly seen, reacts on the
life of the seer. How to live. How to get the most out
of life. How to extract its honey out of the flower of
the world. That is my every day business." And later,
in May of 1853, looking outward to summer, he wrote,
"He is richest who has most use for nature as raw material of tropes and symbols with which to describe
his life. . . . If I am overflowing with life, am rich in
experience for which I lack expression, then nature

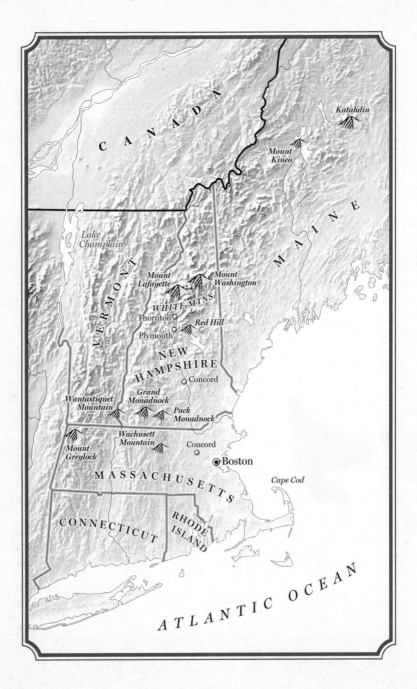

will be my language full of poetry." That same year, at the age of thirty-six, he concluded, "I cannot but regard it as a kindness in those who have the steering of me, by the want of pecuniary wealth, I have been nailed down to this my native region so long and steadily, and made to study and love this spot of earth more and more."

In those few phrases, Thoreau provides a clue to the great concerns of his life: his turning toward field and hill, his belief that in nature lay the great symbols of a well-chosen life, and his deep attachment to and knowledge of place. These sentiments inform both the village life of the young Concord resident and the mountain sensibilities of the fellow who would range far and wide in the high country. To understand the enthusiast of high ground that Thoreau became is to understand, first, that no matter what you've heard, Henry David Thoreau was no homebody. The careful husbandry of Walden aside, Thoreau was a dedicated wanderer. This philosopher, naturalist, house builder, botanist, and leading transcendentalist could not confine himself to the limits of village life, though his local ties were lasting. He kept a chair outside his cabin door but did not linger there, waiting for the world to come to him. Many of his important conversations with Emerson, Channing, Alcott, Hawthorne, and others occurred on long walks in the country. The vastly simplified home life he crafted for himself at Walden Pond was, after all, a means to an end. It freed him to wander as he pleased.

When home, Thoreau was self-employed as a land surveyor and as the erstwhile operator of his family's pencil-making business. In the Concord, Massachusetts, area many household, woodlot, and town boundaries still bear the marks of his well-respected surveys 150 years ago. But though he was an innovator in both trades, these were occasional occupations. His heart and intellect resided elsewhere. He lived to be out and about, first in the woodlands, hills, and dunes of Massachusetts and then in the mountainous backcountry of New Hampshire and Maine. He roamed widely, becoming a connoisseur of his immediate rural countryside and then a habitué of New England's most prominent elevations.

What prompted Thoreau to exchange his village for the mountains, keeping a foot in both worlds? His trips to peak country had many sources of motivation, some of which will be familiar to anyone who values the natural world and the hills that crown it. As the lines quoted earlier show, he derived inspiration from being in the natural world and, as we will see, found in his high-country explorations a source of meaning. Mountains alter perspective and, in a practical sense, show us terrain, flora, and fauna unlike those found at home. The wild roughness captivated him. As Thoreau understood, there is, too, a kind of poetry in natural places. In the woods and hills, there lay simplicity, an order of things primeval and unspoiled. The mountains also offered abundant experience and interest for a poor fellow with a scientific bent. Here was wealth of another sort, and to pass one's days in hill country was no mere idling.

A tireless walker and long-distance hiker, Thoreau developed a lifelong passion for meandering cross-country through woods and hills in the Northeast. His mountain journeys farther afield were a natural outgrowth of his wanderings in the Bay State. He became as familiar as anyone alive with his home counties and then turned to greater challenges. He rowed, walked, sailed, canoed, rode in wagons, and eventually boarded the early steam trains that ran north and west, a traveler in search of the mountains.

A prototypical regional explorer, Thoreau roamed Maine's North Woods and the remoteness of Cape Cod, looking always for the transcendent and the exceptional. He made an art of his tramping. He wrote, "I have met but one or two persons in the course of my life who understood the art of Walking, that is, of taking walks,—who had a genius, so to speak, for sauntering." Now, after a century and a half, Thoreau remains America's most influential commentator on journeying to the mountains and backcountry, then returning home all the wiser. Over our shoulders, we hear Thoreau intoning, "In wildness is the preservation of the world." With this volume as a guide, it is time to go see what he meant.

The genius for sauntering of which Thoreau spoke, of being drawn to the hill country on foot, of climbing the hills that beckoned and sensing that his own place was in those remote locales, will be familiar to anyone who hikes. We recognize at once the urge to leave the settled world behind, to experience nature firsthand, to find our way to high places. An appetite for the natural world runs beyond mere diversion or escape. Thoreau knew something more significant was at stake. Expeditions of this sort feed the mind and the soul, rejuvenating one's sense of being vitally alive in the natural world.

"I think that I cannot preserve my health and spirits unless I spend four hours a day at least—and it is commonly more than that—sauntering through the woods and over the hills and fields, absolutely free from all worldly engagements," he remarked. If you walk or hike because you *must*, because there can be no better way to spend the day, then you understand

Thoreau's impulse. It is this explorer of the Northeast's higher summits, this chronicler of their biological, social, and geological reality, this diarist and self-taught naturalist, whom we join in these pages. Our focus is on Thoreau at large and alert in hill country—where he went, what he did, what he experienced, what he learned, and what he tells us about such moments. This volume is not meant to be a literary enterprise. Thoreau's declarations are best understood by walking the very same hills he investigated. These pages are an invitation to ascend *with* Thoreau, to experience even today that high terrain he found important and inspiring.

There is both insight and pleasure, I think, in following Thoreau to the mountains, and in these pages are specific, present-day commentary and directions to the hills he favored. Trails that Thoreau walked on or near are identified, and descriptions of each journey are provided. Maps included here show the approximate routes Thoreau hiked, some of them little changed today. Thoreau's own comments on his progress will accompany you as you walk, as will details about his life, his moment in American life, and his era. You can also compare notes with Thoreau on how to equip yourself for mountain walks, how to live simply in the high country, how to travel light, and what is essential when you take to the hills.

Thoreau's mountain journeys reveal the explorer in him, a man fully alive in hill country, and one hungry for whatever the alpine atmosphere might impart. In using this guide, you will, I hope, see the mountains as Thoreau saw them. Driven in his time by a continuing desire to see how Nature might reveal herself, Thoreau has become today our most articulate voice urging appreciation of the natural world up close. Ultimately, he went to the hills in pursuit of still another, exceptional universe, worthy of exploration yet apart from the village, a world of high places. And now, with this guide in your rucksack, it is your turn to follow him.

Preface

Thoreau in the Mountains

———◆———

It is worthwhile to see the *Mts* in the horizon
once a day. I have thus seen some earth which
corresponds to my least earthly & trivial—to
my most heavenward looking thoughts—The
earth seen through an azure an etherial veil.
They are the natural *temples* elevated brows of
the earth—looking at which the thoughts of
the beholder are naturally elevated and etheri-
alized. . . . *Mts* thus seen are worthy of worship.

—JOURNAL, SEPTEMBER 12, 1851

Much has been written about Henry David
Thoreau, particularly about his residence in
his native Concord and his two years at Walden Pond.
Some have approached Thoreau from an academic
stance, doing the useful work of establishing texts.
(Thoreau was a frequent rewriter, reuser of episodes,

and editor, and not above cut and paste.) Others have remarked on the philosophical Thoreau and his connections with such leading figures of New England transcendentalism as Emerson, Alcott, Brownson, Fuller, and Ripley, all of whom at times thought Thoreau doctrinally unreliable. Some modern commentators have ignored Thoreau's uncanny multiplicity of skills, only to label him impractical. Others have emphasized the familiar (if often misread) Thoreau of Walden, seeing him as a quaint, hermitlike, cranky fixture of the woods south of Concord, one who, when careless, might set those woods on fire.

Another, essential, Thoreau exists, however, a figure who wandered widely, who became a connoisseur of the regional backcountry, and who on numerous occasions was a habitué of the mountains. This less heralded Thoreau would define New England's remote high places in a broader scheme of things through direct experience. It is this explorer of the Northeast's highest summits, this chronicler of their biological, boreal, and geological reality, this diarist and self-taught naturalist, whom we shall go hiking with in these pages.

Thoreau made more than twenty mountain excursions in his short life. Some lay closer to home, such as his early reconnoiter of Wachusett Mountain and his later visit to Mount Greylock. Others took him over a variety of favorite lower hills in central Massachusetts, southwestern New Hampshire, and, more than once, the outer reaches of Cape Cod. His most worthy expeditions took him to New Hampshire's Grand Monadnock, where he camped several times at altitude, to the Granite State's vast Presidential and Franconia Ranges, and to Maine's Mount Katahdin, Mount Kineo, and remote North Woods. In these excursions, we can see Thoreau growing as a skilled nat-

> As the light increased
> I discovered around me an ocean of mist,
> which by chance reached up to exactly the base
> and shut out every vestige of the earth,
> while I was left floating on this fragment
> of the wreck of the world,
> on my carved plank in cloudland;
> a situation which required
> no aid from the imagination
> to render it impressive.
>
> *Henry David Thoreau*
>
> ...ference to a visit to Mount Greylock from
> *A Week on the Concord and Merrimack River*

Summit stone on Mount Greylock featuring a passage from Thoreau's book A Week on the Concord and Merrimack Rivers

uralist, geographer, geologist, and reporter on the alpine environment. He is also at such moments a hiker and mountaineer of exceptional energy. Thoreau's is a hands-on ethic, too, the idea made concrete, the divine made evident in every tree, river, marsh, or mountain. One had to be there, he thought. And one could expect great joy in looking closely.

Thoreau, as his trips to high places show, was a devotee of the specific. He could not accept the world as a mere mental representation, the countryside as a hazy extension of an idea, of the mind. The natural world was not a mere stage painting, a backdrop. His was an appetite for the real. In the mountains, he believed, there lay an exceptional kind of experience. Elevation brought its own fabulous reality. He would speak of such connections even as he climbed his chosen hills. Thoreau turned intentionally to mountain places outside the day-to-day ken of his fellow residents of Concord and set to capturing the real physical, spiritual, and intellectual meaning of untrammeled high places. He sought to read the very ground.

There were alpine realities that he might examine, touch, make sense of. There was virtue in knowing the real thing, a virtue he pursued again and again in New England's mountains. In the Great White Hills he aimed to catalogue every alpine flower and shrub he could find, and he gathered mountain perspectives as if they were forever worth saving. These views were eventually passed on to his readers. He became a collector of plant and mineral specimens found in remote high ground, later providing these materials to such august persons as the renowned naturalist Louis Agassiz at Harvard. His specimen case, used on shorter expeditions, was his roomy straw hat.

Thoreau lived as an observant fellow of his own village, despite decamping to Walden for a time as a place to "live deliberately." A connected citizen of Concord, he embraced that locale more heartily than we have often been urged to think. Why, then, did he often exchange that village for the mountains? In fact, Thoreau's trips to mountain places had many sources of motivation. In a typical journey he observed many bird species, comparing them with those he saw at home in Concord. He investigated forest growth and followed geological structures to see where they originated. He explored, observed, and identified distant peaks and ranges; went fishing; classified flower and plant species; and, ultimately, interpreted what it all might mean. There were few better at explaining the look of preindustrial America than he.

In taking to the hills, Thoreau became what author Christopher Lenney has called a "sightseeker" or "above-ground archaeologist" of unique places. "Sightseeking, briefly defined, is a systematic sightseeing, and sightseeing is but each traveler's highly conditioned manner of looking at the world," Lenney says. "Sightseeking is underpinned by a wealth of specific references to both things and places. . . . Much of the pleasure of landscape study derives from an appreciation of the tightly-woven texture of the obvious." And so it was with Thoreau. He set out for high ground seeking those larger truths and the compelling beauty in the obvious that others failed to see. His artifacts were not built or social, but natural, often unique and timeless as he found them in the greater hills. He would come to know the nature of his world intimately, would become a true sightseeker, rejecting the obsessive getting and spending of his neighbors for something more universal.

As a wandering outdoorsman, Thoreau confined his compass almost entirely to central and northern New England and New York. Within this region, however, he examined his world closely, registered its texture, listened to its winds, navigated its rivers, and walked out in pursuit of its higher ground. For Thoreau, taking to the hills amounted to something much more than mere exercise. He looked upon the farther reaches of the Northeast as a zone of exploration. In the mid-1800s he found that high places were a platform from which he could see the New England landscape in a new way. Mountaintops themselves were fascinating places. Summit views offered something

MOUNT KTAADN from W. BUTTERFIELD'S
Near the GRAND SCHOODIC LAKE

Katahdin from Butterfield's farm and tavern   Maine State Museum Collections

like a living map. Looking out from a summit ledge, he thought, one might put a whole region in perspective.

There were notable challenges to being a person at large in the Northeast's far corners. Exploring a chosen elevation often meant undertaking a lengthy journey by river and dirt lane before beginning a climb, canoeing a vast waterway such as Moosehead Lake, or setting out on a long-distance, cross-country bushwhacking adventure . Thoreau's expedition to Katahdin, for example, shows us just how much difficult backcountry travel, river and lake, he would willingly undertake to explore so impressive an elevation. His approach to the mountain was earlier preceded by steamship travel northward on the Bangor packet. He sometimes followed rivers north and then hiked up to the ravines and summits where they began, as he did on his first ascent of New Hampshire's Mount Washington in 1839. When the railroads moved past his cabin at Walden, he became an enthusiastic rider to the mountains he valued in southwestern New Hampshire. And then there were the hikes he undertook in central and western Massachusetts and eastern New York by simply walking to the mountains, however distant from Concord.

When Thoreau took to the roads, he made a surprising range of choices as to what he carried with him. Sometimes he placed books in his pack or satchel, preferring to read Virgil in the mountains. At other times he traveled light, philosophizing, "I have traveled thus some hundreds of miles without taking any meal in a house, sleeping on the ground when convenient, and found it cheaper, and in many respects more profitable, than staying at home." He carried items that could do double duty, such as the canvas sail he and his brother, John, rigged on the *Musketaquid* as they traveled north on the Merrimack River. The sail became their tent on evenings ashore. His hat, the interior of which contained a "shelf," became a place to store small specimens collected along the way. A small hatchet was useful for cutting firewood, garnering spruce or fir brush to sleep on, pounding tent stakes, and many other things.

Taken to extremes, Thoreau had a formula for carrying astonishingly little while walking cross-country. He believed that "the cheapest way to travel, and the way to travel the shortest distance, is to go afoot, carrying a dipper, a spoon, and a fishline, some Indian meal, some salt, and some sugar. When you come to a brook or pond, you can catch fish and cook them; or you can boil a hasty-pudding; or you can buy a loaf of bread at a farmer's house for fourpence, moisten it in the next brook that crosses the road and dip into it your sugar—this alone will last you a whole day; or, if you are accustomed to heartier living, you can buy a quart of milk for two cents, crumb your bread or cold pudding into it, and eat it with your own spoon out of your own dish."

Thoreau described himself as "plucking the raspberries by the wayside" on his way to Mount Greylock and "carrying a knapsack on my back which held a few traveler's books and a change of clothing." In North Adams he paused to add "a little rice and sugar, and a tin cup into my knapsack." This is minimalism indeed, foraging for wild fruit, obtaining what he needed from the land and from locals as he walked, and living rough. Certainly he had devised a means of improvising his way along country roads and into the hills. The contrast between Thoreau's method and the relative comforts of high-tech backpacking today is considerable.

Thoreau rarely speaks in his writing of taking along specialized clothing or outerwear when hiking, apparently not giving it much thought. At a number of points he seems to accept getting wet and found that he could dry out quickly when resuming a walk in the sun. He preferred brief showers of short duration, as he noted in his journal in 1852: "Caught in a thunder-shower south of Flint's Pond. Stood under thick trees. I care not how hard it rains, if it does not rain more than 15 minutes. I can shelter myself effectively in the woods."

Carrying a blanket while camping at altitude was only an occasional practice for Thoreau. His comments about sleeping under some boards on a summit have been dismissed as a kind of rascal primitivism by some. He mentions using a tent on Wachusett and in Tuckerman Ravine on Mount Washington, but tents seem to have been an appliance useful only when traveling with one or more other people. In some circumstances at elevation he routinely fashioned his own shelter, usually by constructing a lean-to.

An interesting exception to this frugal, ultrasimple style of tramping was Thoreau's second visit to Mount Washington in 1858. He was invited to ride to the North Country with his friend and sometime fellow hiker Edward Hoar, who had hired a horse and cart. Since this was a trip where one might bring along a luxurious plenty of hiking gear and supplies, Thoreau created a long list of things he thought ideal for such an extended high-altitude expedition. When the twosome left their horse and cart north of New Hampshire's Pinkham Notch, a man from Jackson was hired to pack their supplies up the mountain.

Thoreau's list of mountaineering essentials for this second journey to the Presidential Range contained thirty-five items (or groups of items), large and small. Since he and Hoar planned to do as extensive a survey of alpine plant species as they could, Thoreau's lengthy list was perhaps influenced by his intended scientific collecting. (They were in search of forty-six species they had identified as likely inhabitants of the mountain's alpine zone.) In any case, his gear on this trip was strikingly different from his usual pack contents.

For clothing, Thoreau later recommended:
Three strong check shirts
Two pairs socks
Neck ribbon and handkerchief
Three pocket-handkerchiefs
One thick waistcoat
One thin (or half-thick) coat
One thick coat (for mountain)
A flannel shirt
India-rubber coat
Three bosoms (to go and come in)
A cap to lie in at night

The sheer bulk and weight of this outfit would, of course, fill a very large pack and weigh at least twenty to twenty-five pounds. But there was more. Thoreau specified a blanket and a two-man tent for comfort, as well as a number of items to support his botanizing. They included:

A map and compass
Plant book and paper
Paper and stamps
Botany spyglass, microscope
Tape, insect-boxes
Jack-knife and clasp-knife
Veil and gloves

For his kitchen and larder, Thoreau included:
Fish-line and hooks
Matches
Soap and dish-cloths
Waste-paper and twine

A napkin
Pins, needle and thread
Iron spoon
Pint dipper with a pail-handle added
And perhaps a bag to carry water in
Frying pan, only if you ride
Hatchet (sharp) if you ride
And perhaps in any case on a mountain
with a sheath to it
Hard-bread (sweet crackers good)
A moist sweet plum-cake very good and lasting
Pork, corned beef or tongue
Sugar
Tea or coffee
And a little salt

We may safely assume that Thoreau most often preferred to travel light and cover ground rapidly when hiking cross-country. He appears to have dared himself to get by with little in the way of creature comforts and to have enjoyed the challenge. It was another way of expressing impatience with the trappings of the larger culture. He would, in most circumstances, be a minimalist. But as his longer Mount Washington expedition list indicates, he might sometimes have chosen a more extensive kit when he had a conveyance available and the need to carry more. On the journey mentioned, there was, too, the fact of traveling with or meeting others in the high country. On this Mount Washington survey, friends joined him in Tuckerman Ravine, hollering their hellos from the headwall. As a result, five people were sheltered in his two-man tent on the ravine floor, and all had to be fed.

Thoreau was, by any measure, an unconventional hiker. He walked across country, often across lots, following routes of his own devising. He was sometimes familiar with the landscape in a way that its owners were not. Quite often when in hill country he would spy a high peak in the distance and then proceed toward it, making a beeline for its summit. Once on a mountain he would explore the mountain itself and its subsidiaries. He made clear that he wanted to look at the mountain, not just its views. He would camp on summits, sometimes sleeping rough in makeshift shelters or lean-tos of his own making. In remote places where at least rudimentary trails or paths existed, Thoreau would often make his own way up through the woods, by choice covering very rugged and more difficult ground because the route was more direct. His ascent of Maine's Mount Katahdin is a perfect example. Though a primitive trail reached Katahdin's highest point in 1846, Thoreau led his party instead on a bushwhacking trek over an adjacent col and then up almost impassable, steep terrain, along stream channels, and through tangled blowdown to the mountain's summit plateau. He was no complainer, but his journal makes clear just how difficult the ascent and descent of Katahdin actually was off-trail.

Whatever his habits when at large in the hills, Thoreau's motivation for going, for transporting himself to the woods, hills, and mountains, found its beginnings in a unique way of looking at the world. In July of 1845, when he took up residence in his cabin at Walden Pond, he wrote, "I wish to meet the facts of life—the vital facts, which are the phenomena or actuality the gods meant to show us—face to face, and so I came down here." Seven years later he observed, "By my intimacy with Nature I find myself withdrawn from man. My interest in the sun and moon, in the morning and evening, compels me to solitude." And a few months later, in January of 1853, the idea apparently still on his mind, he clarified his thinking further. "I love nature partly because she is not man, but a retreat from him. None of his institutions control or pervade her. There a different kind of right prevails. In her midst I can be glad with an entire gladness."

These sentiments do not make Thoreau antisocial—there is plenty of evidence to the contrary—but instead define a man who had a visceral need for the natural world, for the perfection of wild places. He was certainly reflective about his deeprooted predilection for walking in the wild. At many points in his writing, he speaks directly of the connection between being much in the natural world and his own mental and physical health. In November of 1852 he concluded, "[I] Must be out-of-doors enough to get experience of wholesome reality, as a balance to thought and sentiment. Health requires this relaxation, this aimless life. This life in the present. . . . I keep out of doors for the sake of the mineral, vegetable and animal in me." Anyone who follows Thoreau to the mountains today might comfortably subscribe to these same views.

As he made his way to hill country, Thoreau found nature to be sublime, transcendent. It is the one well into which we can dip again and again and never go home thirsty, he thought. In the woods the spirit is mended and given drink that is clear

> *"Health requires this relaxation, this aimless life. This life in the present. . . . I keep out of doors for the sake of the mineral, vegetable and animal in me."*

and cold. In July of 1845, using the cabin at Walden as his new base, he observed, "What sweet and tender, the most innocent and divinely encouraging society there is in every natural object, and so in universal nature, even for the poor misanthrope and most melancholy man! There can be no really black melancholy to him who lives in the midst of Nature and still has his senses."

Taken as a whole, Thoreau's hill country wanderings illustrate his intense interest in the flora, fauna, silviculture, and geology of the mountains he visited. What he learned about these things became part of the greater journey of his life. These discoveries resulted in a careful recording of what he encountered, ranging from short notes to long, highly detailed essays on different plant and tree species, rock formations, birds, and animals. An excellent illustration of his natural history gleanings from his mountaineering and other walks appears in writing done between 1850 and his death in 1862. Left unfinished as a collection at Thoreau's passing, and now available in the sublime *Wild Fruits,* edited by Bradley Dean, are Thoreau's comments on plants and fruits he examined. "The value of these wild fruits is not in the mere possession or eating of them," he noted, "but in the sight and enjoyment of them."

Among many longer themes in *Wild Fruits* are Thoreau's thoughts on the pleasant subject of blueberries and their presence both in mountain country and on his native turf. Thinking probably about his Monadnock excursions, he remembered, "In many New Hampshire towns a neighboring mountaintop is the common berry field of many villages, and in the berry season such a summit will be swarming with pickers. . . . When camping on such ground, thinking myself quite out of the world, I have had my solitude very unexpectedly invaded by an army of this description—some even making their way up there thro' the morning fog before sunrise, shouting and thumping their pails in order that they might keep together—and I found that the weekdays were the only sabbath days there at that season."

His comments on blueberries are extensive and recurring. He chronicled the characteristics of the different varieties he found and their presence at various altitudes and in different settings, from central and western Massachusetts to the northern Maine woods and Katahdin. His remarks make fair distinctions among various subspecies and their distribution. (He often counted on berrying to form part of his diet when he was hiking with minimal provisions.) Northern New England berrying in hill country is still a custom for a dwindling number of enthusiasts who, like Thoreau, have come to make similar distinctions as to taste, variety, and location. Thoreau's notes on the subject would be as good a guide for any hiker in search of this kind of refreshment today as when they were written. (One does not, however, give away the secret of where the densest, most productive berry patches are found.)

As mentioned earlier, other transcendentalists thought Thoreau suspicious. After all, he did not dwell on or fuss over theoretical or philosophical niceties and seemed focused always on the concrete, the immutable, in this life. Thoreau was, I think, the more genuine specimen of transcendental living in his time. Emerson, who more than any was his mentor, often grew impatient with him. Thoreau cared nothing for doctrine and frequently found it repugnant. His church lay out of doors in field and hill. If perfection could be found anywhere in Thoreau's universe, it resided not in doctrine, but in river valleys, deep woods, and mountains. Emerson seems not to have fully comprehended or accepted this about his pupil until, perhaps, the end.

If one reads Thoreau extensively, especially his day-to-day assays of the woodlands within his reach, a certain injunction occurs again and again: Pay attention! His responses to the natural world are both spiritual and practical, expressions of both the inner and outer self. He had, it becomes clear, not much patience for those who couldn't see the natural world beyond the counting box. He makes the observation in one essay that a community might be blessed with great natural beauty yet not enjoy it because so much public disconnect with raw nature prevailed. He spoke for intention, both in his writing and through his actions, by going to the woods and hills.

In October of 1859, out cranberrying at Gowing's Swamp in Concord, Thoreau observed, "Many of our days should be spent, not in vain expectations, and lying on our oars, but in carrying out deliberately and faithfully the hundred little purposes which every man's genius must have suggested to him." Go forth, act on inspiration, and have a plan, he seems to say. And later, "Both a conscious and an unconscious life are good; neither is good exclusively, for both have the same source. The wisely conscious life springs out of an unconscious suggestion. I have found my account when traveling in having prepared beforehand a list of questions which I would get answered, not trusting to my interest at the moment, and can then travel with most profit." Here is inspiration leading to intent leading to a plan of action leading to attentive involvement. All of this, he intimates, makes us better, more intense observers in the field, on the mountain, wherever. Inspiration carries us to insight. "It is by obeying the suggestions of a higher light within you that you escape from yourself and, in the transit, as it were see with the unworn sides of your eye, travel totally new paths." To connect with the terrain, we must listen to inspiration, give it our full attention, examine it with intent, and make our way to higher ground. Spirit, intellect, and the observant eye respond to nature as one—rather good advice for mountain travel (or walking anywhere in the natural world) in an age when some run up and down mountains to brag about speed, missing just about everything.

> "*Many of our days should be spent, not in vain expectations, and lying on our oars, but in carrying out deliberately and faithfully the hundred little purposes which every man's genius must have suggested to him.*"

All his days, Thoreau held true to this attentive impulse toward nature, to remaining an intentional explorer of the earth's rough places. He became uncomfortable at times even as a surveyor, out making a living, fearing it reduced his sensitivity to natural things. The modern world is full of suggestions as to how Thoreau might have lived or should have lived. He was originally believed by some in his own village to be a loafer, but he knew better. His life, especially in the hills, was well crafted and right. He knew what he was meant to do and was always busy at it. In March of 1853 he said, "It is essential that a man confine himself to pursuits . . . which lie next to and conduce to his life, which do not go against the grain, either of his will or imagination. . . . Dwell as near as possible to the channel in which your life flows." And so he did.

1. Mount Washington
(WEST)
The Southern Presidentials

————◦•◦————

As it is important to consider Nature from the point of view of science, remembering the nomenclature and system of men, and so, if possible, go a step further in that direction, so it is equally important often to ignore or forget all that men presume that they know, and take an original and unprejudiced view of Nature, letting her make what impression she will on you, as the first men, and all children and natural men still do. For our science, so called, is always more barren and mixed up with error than our sympathies are.

—JOURNAL, FEBRUARY 28, 1860

There they stood, the two of them, two brothers, one pushing, the other pulling, something resembling a skiff, yet strangely equipped with wheels.

This was the launch of the *Musketaquid*, and the brothers were not alone. A noisy collection of enthusiasts from the village of Concord had turned out to be helpful witnesses to the commencement of a great enterprise. The year was 1839.

John, a schoolmaster, and his younger brother, Henry David, not long out of John Harvard's little college for divines, were exerting themselves in the name of adventure. After a winter of planning, the two had constructed, out of local timber, the *Musketaquid*, a sixteen-foot dorylike rowboat, which they had further equipped with a mast and crude sail. The sail would double as a tent. Inspiration had led to the addition of a set of wheels as a means, such as the moment called for, by which the craft could be rolled around falls, dams, and over portages. Though not a yacht certainly, the sturdy craft was meant to carry the brothers north on the Concord and Merrimack Rivers to the farthest reaches of New Hampshire's White Mountains. It would not disappoint them.

Though this journey would become known to the world in print as a river trip, it was, in fact, a prelude to the brothers' assault on New England's most prominent mountains. The two envisioned a firsthand reconnoiter of New Hampshire's legendary Great White Hills and the Northeast's tallest mountain range. They would advance to the headwaters of the Pemigewasset and Ammonoosuc Rivers. Their ultimate destination would be the second-highest summit east of the Mississippi, which they would approach via the southern Presidential Range. Over meals in the family household in Concord, the younger Thoreau had talked about reaching the Ammonoosuc's mountain headwaters: They would go in search of riverine beginnings. In rivers there were stories, thought young Henry, and at their head lay great mountains. This was to be a journey deeper in.

The little expedition was the first of many Henry David Thoreau would make to remote mountain places over the next twenty years. He had chosen New England's highest summit for starters and would return later to the Presidential Range to comment more directly on his mountain observations, which were many. For now, those mountains lay 170 miles distant, and the brothers had ribbons of river to row. And row they did. Firing a small gun in a celebratory salute, the two cast off, pointing the *Musketaquid* up the Concord River and feeling almost instantly a remove from the life of the community of which they were normally a part.

For two days the pair proceeded north, paddling through locks and into the Merrimack. In his journal Henry warmed to remote farms that were now and then visible from the river. These rural outposts pleased him, signs of a simple, almost idyllic life in New England's midst. Approaching Concord, New Hampshire, the brothers erected a rudimentary tent with their sail and spent the night in a Hooksett farmer's field, awaking to the stares of inquisitive cattle. Rain descended, and the twosome asked to leave their humble boat in the willing farmer's barn, to be reclaimed on their return journey. There were falls ahead and another lock at Bow, through which they judged it too difficult to navigate.

The brothers hiked from their Hooksett campsite to Concord, where, after a night's stay, they boarded a northbound stage. Their route wound through New Hampshire's pretty lake country and then northwest to the little academy town of Plymouth, the last community of any size below the White

Mountains. What had begun as a leisurely river odyssey was about to become a trek dependent on shank's mare. Plymouth was the last community of any size before the travelers stepped outside the settled world and made for the mountains that awaited them.

Thoreau's journal indicates that they shouldered their packs and walked north on the gravel cart track that followed the Pemigewasset River toward the imposing granite notches that lay above. Here the real work began. Over the next several days, the two would walk more than eighty miles in increasingly demanding terrain. And once in the high country, they would not only gather miles but also ascend thousands of feet, capturing a whole range of lofty elevations. The speed with which they covered the hill country remains impressive even today. Although Thoreau would later mine his journal and other notes to pen *A Week on the Concord and Merrimack Rivers,* his book about the river passage, the mountains ahead were the pair's real, intended challenge, terrain new to both. The Great White Hills, the fountainhead that shaped the rivers they had been following, was now within reach.

By nightfall of the first day, the brothers had fast-marched to the foothill community of Thornton, where they took lodgings. "We no longer sailed or floated on the river, but trod the unyielding land like pilgrims," Thoreau wrote. "True and sincere traveling is no pastime, but it is as serious as the grave, or any part of the human journey, and it requires a long probation to be broken into it." As they continued hiking north the next morning, they found their way between two great mountain ranges, these highlands ranging north and northeast on either side of the Pemigewasset. These first elevations were a tangle of lower summits. To the west lay the distinctive, rounded shapes of Mount Kineo, Mount Cilley, and Grandview Mountain, a prelude to the loftier shapes that awaited the travelers to the north. Farther up-land they would see Mount Pemige-wasset, the long line of Kinsman Ridge, and, at the head of Franconia Notch, the bold, naked cliffs of Can-non Mountain. This range even now stands rugged and beautiful, a classic alpine perspective where hikers and rock climbers can be discovered at play.

> *"True and sincere traveling is no pastime, but it is as serious as the grave, or any part of the human journey, and it requires a long probation to be broken into it."*

Continuing north along the east side of the intervening valley, the Thoreaus passed intermediate summits 1,700 to 2,800 feet in elevation. As they walked beneath the first of these higher summits, they paused and made their way up the rough, boulder-strewn natural cleft on the east side of the notch known today as the Flume. A bold fissure created by moving water, weathering, synclinal pressure, and ice, the Flume exposes the rocky innards of these hills. The scramble today is made on a network of wooden walkways, an easier ascent than the one the brothers made over primitive log bridges. Henry would later write of a stone pool he saw here, a basin carved in the granitic rock by thousands of years of falling water. Eventually his sister Sophia would come here, too, and record her impressions as well.

Closer to the height of the notch, the two hiked past Little and Big Coolidge Mountains and Mounts Flume, Liberty, Lin-coln, and Lafayette. The latter four majestic peaks, at elevations

Mount Lafayette (left), Mount Lincoln, and Little Haystack

from 4,300 to more than 5,200 feet, form a rugged eastern wall that supports the Franconia Ridge Trail, a section of the 2,200-mile-long Appalachian Trail. The brothers did not climb in either of these opposing ranges—the Kinsmans and Lafayette Ridge—on this trip, although Henry made several comments on natural features here in his journal. He would return here years later to climb the highest of the Franconia Ridge peaks, windswept Mount Lafayette, and to botanize around the tiny Eagle Lakes near where the Appalachian Mountain Club's Greenleaf Hut stands today.

Of their progress north Thoreau wrote, "Suns rose and set and found us still on the dank forest path which meanders up the Pemigewassett, now more like an otter's or a marten's trail, or where a beaver had dragged his trap, than where the wheels of travel raise a dust; where towns begin to serve as gores, only to hold the earth together. . . . The very yards of our hostelries inclined upon the skirts of mountains, and, as we passed, we looked up at a steep angle at the systems of maples waving in the clouds."

Hiking beneath these two ranges, the brothers gained nearly 1,500 feet in elevation while traversing an increasingly steep valley floor. The brutal, weeping rock of the Cannon Cliffs loomed to the west. The brothers paused to view intact Whittier's "Great Stone Face," as Thoreau noted in his journal. The cliffs are today minus the millennial rock countenance of the Old Man of the Mountain, which collapsed and plunged into the rubble at their base. The men shortly reached the highest point over which they would walk that day. Traversing the height of land between Eagle Cliff and Cannon Mountain, they passed Mirror Lake and descended to the small, northern village of Franconia, nestled in an intervale five miles to the northwest. They had covered roughly twenty steep and demanding miles since leaving Thornton earlier that day, on top of their fifteen-mile walk north from Plymouth the day before.

If the headwaters of the Pemigewasset and the Ammonoosuc were their ultimate objective, the brothers had taken the long way around by coming through Franconia Notch. Ascending through Crawford Notch would have been considerably more direct, if farther from the tangle of rivers they'd been following. The price of staying with the rivers was that they still had a considerable distance to travel before they could ascend Mount Washington.

The Ammonoosuc, which feeds the Pemigewasset, rises high in a steep ravine of the same name between Mounts

Monroe and Washington, near the center of New Hampshire's Presidential Range. Runoff from the high col that links the two summits, the site of the Lakes of the Clouds, is augmented by a large network of alpine brooks plunging northward. The lakes, actually two shallow glacial tarns, may be seen today and provide a water supply to the AMC's Lakes of the Clouds Hut. By the time these consolidated threads of water reach Bretton Woods, the river is a rocky, energetic series of falls and channels that pull westward. During spring runoff or after a rain, the stream develops some of the most impressive hidden, nonnavigable rapids in New Hampshire's North Country. Now and then, at quieter moments, there are rumors of trout.

Later, in *A Week*, Thoreau would explain the river sequence they were following: "The Merrimack, or Sturgeon River, is formed by the confluence of the Pemigewasset, which rises near the Notch of the White Mountains, and the Winnipiseogee, which drains the lake of the same name." Though Thoreau does not mention it there, the Pemigewasset was, of course, fed by the rough Ammonoosuc, with which the brothers would shortly become acquainted. He would later write, "I have traced its stream [the Merrimack] from where it bubbles out of the rocks of the White Mountains above the clouds, to where it is lost amid the salt billows of the ocean on Plum Island Beach. . . . At first it comes on murmuring to itself by the base of the stately and retired mountains, through moist primitive woods, whose juices it receives, where the bear still drinks it and the cabins of settlers are far between and there are few to cross its stream."

They had come a long way. But now, to connect with the Ammonoosuc and those summits where it forms, the brothers would have to hike northeasterly along a route probably close to present-day NH 142, skirting Mount Agassiz and Cleveland Mountain. They turned more to the east then and apparently crossed the Ammonoosuc at Pierce Bridge, where Thoreau commented on the stream in his journal. He mocked the river's narrow course here, calling it "puny," and noted, "Wandering on through the notches which the streams had made, by the side and over the brows of hoar hills and mountains, across the stumpy, rocky, forested, and bepastured country, we at length crossed on prostrate trees over the Amonoosuck and breathed the free air of Unappropriated Land."

> *"Wandering on through the notches which the streams had made, we at length crossed on prostrate trees over the Amonoosuck and breathed the free air of Unappropriated Land."*

Although Thoreau doesn't note the brothers' exact course from there to the Presidentials, researchers have shown convincingly that they followed the river east for several miles and then turned more southeast to Fabyan, recrossing the river at Giant's Grave. From there they ascended south up further grades on a cart track to the height of land in Crawford Notch. This narrow, high notch between Mount Clinton (now Pierce) and Mounts Willard, Tom, and Field was then the site of the Notch Inn, situated near Saco Pond and operated by the Crawford family. The Crawfords began settlement, inn keeping, and trail work in the area in the early 1800s, and their legacy endures today. Having walked another twenty-three miles from Franconia, Henry and John Thoreau rested the night and then another day at the Notch Inn, biding their time while awaiting weather clear enough for the very exposed hike across the southern Presidentials to Mount Washington's summit.

The brothers now faced the ultimate test of their energies, the more than eight-mile trek across New England's highest peaks in a zone believed to have some of the worst weather in the Western Hemisphere. (North American record wind velocities of 231 miles per hour have been recorded by weather watchers at the Mount Washington Observatory.) The fit young men had their choice of two routes to Mount Washington, both cut as paths by the Crawfords, who guided occasional travelers to the summits.

The newer trail, opened in 1821, skirted the northern side of the southern Presidentials. It worked its way over rough, wet, spruce-studded land to a steep arm of terrain that ascends to alpine pastures on Mount Washington's north side. The route approached the summit via Mount Clay, skirting the lip of the Great Gulf. Sylvester Marsh would in later years construct a rack, or cog, railway along this steep, broken ridge to the summit. The cog railway base station and the point where the trail originally turned upward is now known as Marshfield. The other route, whose trailhead lay adjacent to the Notch House, had been cut in 1819 and ventured east over Mounts Clinton, Pleasant (now Eisenhower), Franklin, and Monroe to the Lakes of the Clouds and then northeast up the exposed and rocky cone of Mount Washington. There is every indication that the brothers chose this older route, eventually known as the Crawford Path, for their alpine passage. The Crawfords would, in time, widen this path so that guests might ride across the range on horseback.

The Presidentials, a heavily glaciated series of peaks that are part of the Appalachian highlands, lean northeastward across northern New Hampshire before the Appalachians tumble into Maine. These are very old mountains, their base probably formed in the Ordovician, beginning 415 million years ago. During this period Albee formation quartzite, Ammonoosuc volcanics, and intrusions of Highlandcraft magma formed a base nearly five thousand feet thick. In the Devonian the region was covered by an inland sea whose mud, sand, and limestone depositions over hundreds of thousands of years would become the Littleton formation, modified subsequently by heat and pressure into the range's characteristic gneiss, schists, and quartzite. In the Mesozoic more than 130 million years of erosion took place, reshaping the landmass considerably. During the Cenozoic, beginning 60 million years ago, an epoch of weathering, uplift, and erosion occurred, during which this range gained something like its current profile. With the arrival of the colder Pleistocene, hanging glaciers formed in the peaks, and the Wisconsin ice sheet gradually covered the entire area for about 50,000 years. Glaciers scrubbed the range's summits, widened valleys, and left deposits of glacial drift, sands, and pockets of glacial till. The effects of this glaciation were evident in Thoreau's time and are still visible today. He would write about this terrain on a return trip to Mount Washington, which we will follow in chapter 10. Twenty thousand to thirty thousand years ago, melting commenced and the glaciers slowly receded, leaving behind the many glacial erratics found throughout the region. Left behind, too, was a distinctly rugged, rocky, climatically challenged mountain range across which the Thoreau brothers would next walk.

MOUNT WASHINGTON (WEST)
ROUTE DESCRIPTION

The Crawford Path, Thoreau's 1839 route to Mount Washington from the west, begins opposite the AMC's Highland Center at the height of Crawford Notch. The center may be approached on NH 302 from Twin Mountain in the north or on NH 302 via Bartlett and Glen in the south. The Highland Center provides accommodations for hikers, meals, and maps and includes a store where other hiking necessaries may be purchased. For reservations and other information, visit the AMC website, www.outdoors.org. From NH 302 roughly opposite the Highland Center, head northeast on Mount Clinton Road to a parking area reached shortly. Cross the road on foot and follow the Crawford Connector, a path that crosses Gibbs Brook in less than half a mile and, just beyond, reaches the original Crawford Path, established in 1819 and widened in 1840.

The trail now ascends left (northeast) on moderate grades through mixed growth dominated by hardwoods and, above, lichen-draped black spruce. It climbs above Gibbs Brook and passes a short spur at 0.6 mile, which leads left to views of Gibbs Falls. On the Crawford Path, grades begin to steepen somewhat now as the trail pulls away from the brook and to the east and southeast. At just under 2 miles you reach the Mizpah Cutoff on the right. This trail runs about 0.7 mile southeast and east on easy grades to the AMC's Mizpah Spring Hut, where accommodations and meals are available by reservation (www.outdoors.org).

The Crawford Path continues upward, climbing steadily northeast through coniferous growth of shorter stature that shows the

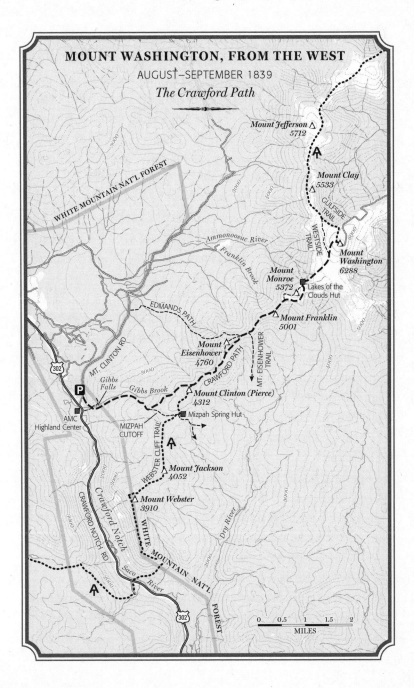

MOUNT WASHINGTON, FROM THE WEST
AUGUST–SEPTEMBER 1839
The Crawford Path

Mount Jefferson △
5712

Mount Clay
5533 △

GULFSIDE TRAIL

WESTSIDE TRAIL

Mount Washington
6288

Ammonoosuc River

Franklin Brook

WHITE MOUNTAIN NAT'L FOREST

Mount Monroe
5372

Lakes of the Clouds Hut

EDMANDS PATH

Mount Franklin
5001

Mount Eisenhower
4760

CRAWFORD PATH

MT. EISENHOWER TRAIL

MT. CLINTON RD

9000

Gibbs Falls

Gibbs Brook

Mount Clinton (Pierce)
4312

302

P

AMC Highland Center

MIZPAH CUTOFF

Mizpah Spring Hut

WEBSTER CLIFF TRAIL

Mount Jackson
4052

Mount Webster
3910

Crawford Notch

CRAWFORD NOTCH RD

WHITE MOUNTAIN NAT'L

Saco River

Dry River

FOREST

302

| 0 | 0.5 | 1 | 1.5 | 2 |

MILES

effects of the punishing winds that rake this area year-round. The path levels somewhat and soon comes into the open near the summit of Mount Pierce (formerly Clinton). Here there is a junction with the Webster Cliff Trail on the right, which leads to Pierce's summit and then descends to Mizpah Spring Hut. Ahead is a true panorama with superb views of the southern Presidential Range and Mount Washington. A number of times I have seen a great undercast here, with all the valleys and lesser summits covered completely by clouds. On New Year's Day 1980, my friends and I paused to eat lunch here in our shirtsleeves, in an extraordinary moment of temperature inversion at a spot that, in winter, is usually dangerously cold.

Even on the best summer day these mountains are subject to strong, persistent winds out of the northwest that often bring severe storms. From this point east to Lakes of the Clouds Hut, there are limited opportunities to get out of the wind by dropping down into patches of scrub. Beyond the hut, the treeless ground looking like lunar rock that forms the shoulder between the lakes and Mount Washington's summit offers no safe shelter.

Orographic cooling occurs as moist air rises over these mountain slopes and condenses along the Crawford Path. The whole range becomes a busy cloud factory. On some days you may walk the whole length of the range immersed in clouds. The highly exposed trail also collects fully formed storms from the northwest, accompanied by rain, sleet, or snow. Sometimes the lacerating winds bring a generous portion of each. The weather here can change abruptly, with very little warning. Hiking this range in a westerly direction, I've occasionally watched compact storm systems miles away approach from the far northwest, only to reach me in a matter of minutes, pushing hail and high winds over the summits. At such moments hikers must find a boulder or two big enough to shelter under if possible. These storms may depart equally quickly, with the sun reappearing. Periodically, vast cloud layers blanket the valleys for hours, rendering hundreds of square miles of lowland invisible to hikers on the ridges.

What the Thoreau brothers encountered in the way of winds here on September 10, 1839, can only be guessed, but it would be the exceptional day if they found mild, settled weather. As researcher Christopher McKee has noted, Henry later destroyed some early journals that covered this summit-to-summit journey, leaving us only cryptic comments on the successful climb. It seems utterly uncharacteristic of him to throw away his notes on this most challenging section of his journey, the moments when he reached his chosen destination, for he husbanded his observations carefully. Still, in some fashion unknown to us in detail, the brothers moved across this range, peak to peak, in whatever weather awaited them.

The Crawford Path continues northeastward, dropping now and again into wooded areas briefly and then ascending onto open ledge marked by stone cairns. Here fine outlooks to the surrounding peaks, both north and south, are found. After crossing a small brook and ascending on more open ledge, the path reaches a junction with the Mount Eisenhower Loop at 4.3 miles. Go right (northeast) on the Crawford Path, where the walking becomes more level and then passes through a wooded area. The Mount Eisenhower Loop, which leads to the Edmands Path, comes back to the Crawford Path on the left soon, by a glacial pan known as Red Pond. The Crawford Path then passes the Mount Eisenhower Trail on the right (south) at 5 miles.

The Crawford Path next slabs upward along the north side of

Mount Franklin above the ravine to the north that carries Franklin Brook. At 5.5 miles it levels off and passes a path to Franklin's summit. Mount Monroe (5,273 feet), with its two distinct summits, appears to the north of the Crawford Path, and at 6.2 miles the Monroe Loop, diverging to the left, leads upward over those peaks and then down to Lakes of the Clouds Hut. The Crawford Path, which is more protected in storms, and the Monroe Loop rejoin at the hut. Lakes of the Clouds Hut is a large accommodation perched on the col between Mount Monroe and Mount Washington, which now dominates the view to the east. (Accommodations and meals are available by reservation at www.outdoors.org.) The hut is completely in the open and is buffeted by winds and storms with regularity. It is at the head of the dramatic ravine where the Ammonoosuc River gathers its waters, dropping northward. Just above the hut, to the southeast, are the two shallow ponds known as the Lakes of the Clouds. In the vicinity of the hut are protected areas where endangered species such as *Potentilla canadensis* (dwarf cinquefoil) are off-limits to hikers. Please use caution and carefully avoid these areas if you walk here.

The final leg of the Thoreaus' 8.5-mile hike from Crawford Notch to Mount Washington's summit begins at the lakes and ascends northeast, passing a junction with the Westside Trail on the left at nearly 8 miles and the Gulfside Trail in another quarter mile, at 6,150 feet. Watch for cairns and paint blazes as you climb here. This section of the Crawford Path lies totally exposed to the weather and can be hazardous on even the mildest summer days. The trail now climbs sharply upward to the northwest corner of Mount Washington's flat, rocky summit and the summit buildings, where it arrives shortly.

Modern-day hikers are left, unfortunately, with the enigma of

Lakes of the Clouds and the southern Presidentials

what the Thoreau brothers actually experienced on their roughly 17-mile alpine walk to and from Crawford Notch to Mount Washington's 6,288-foot apex. This is all the more disappointing because this section of the Thoreaus' journey traversed some of the most spectacular alpine scenery in the East and a whole handful of New Hampshire's highest places. The route the brothers followed offers the only true extended alpine walk in eastern North America consistently above treeline, at elevations of 4,000 to over 6,000 feet. (A similar, but lower and shorter, ridge walk exists on Vermont's Mount Mansfield.) It also continues northeastward beyond Mount Washington, running over Mount Clay, Mount Jefferson, the three summits of Mount Adams, and Mount Madison, all at similar altitudes. These northern Presidential summits are all visible from Mount Washington. The blasted, rocky terrain, often glazed with ice and rime even in summer, demands close attention from hikers, as there have been many injuries and deaths here from accidents and exposure. At such heights, the hike would have been Henry David Thoreau's most ambitious expedition up to this moment in his life.

When the brothers reached Washington's summit, they found an undeveloped place, without buildings or other structures: a rock pile, as it has often been called. (Today a modern summit house with food service and toilets, the Mount Washington Observatory, and radio antennas occupy the spot.) It would be gratifying to know what Henry and John thought of the bare, storm-scoured mountaintop, with its stunning 360-degree views of dozens of other mountains and ranges in three states. Christopher McKee has pointed to a minor reference Henry made to the views in a letter written two years later. He was in the throes of writing poetry then and likened the work before him to viewing range after range of hills as seen from Mount Washington: "Just now I am in the mid-sea of verses. . . . I see the stanzas rise around me, verse upon verse, far and near, like the mountains from Agiocochook, not all having a terrestrial existence as yet, even as some of them may be clouds; but I fancy I see the gleam of some Sebago Lake and Silver Cascade, at whose well I may drink one day." These references are, of course, to landmarks Thoreau may have seen while on Mount Washington's summit. If nothing else, the comment tells us that Thoreau's experience in the Presidential Range touched him deeply, and the view from the summit became a lasting motif in his consciousness. He would return for a closer look years later, as we'll see in chapter 10. For the time being, however, he would turn to other mountains and other journeys closer to home.

Mount Washington Obvservatory and summit house

The return to Crawford Notch is made by retracing the Crawford Path westward, as did the Thoreaus, enjoying a very different set of views on the return hike. *Caution:* If you decide to undertake this long and demanding alpine walk, prepare for challenging weather even if temperatures seem mild and the sun is shining. Carry food, plenty of water, a sweater, gloves, a wind- and rainproof jacket, pants, a hat, and a reliable flashlight. Good-quality hiking boots with Vibram or similar soles are a must. This is not a walk for sneakers or running shoes. Carry this guide, its map, and a compass with you as well. The AMC's current "White Mountains Trail Map: Presidential Range" is also recommended.

Experienced, conditioned hikers can complete the hike up and back in an 8- or 9-hour day. (If you step off the Crawford Path on side trails to the summits of Eisenhower, Franklin, and Monroe, expect it to take longer.) Inexperienced hikers might plan a more leisurely trip, spending the first night at Mizpah Spring Hut and the second night at Lakes of the Clouds Hut, reaching Mount Washington's summit on day three, and then walking the full distance west back to Crawford Notch the same day. It is also possible to take a Mount Washington Auto Road shuttle down Washington's east side to the Glen House or Pinkham Notch Camp, then take an AMC seasonally operated shuttle from Pinkham Notch Camp to Crawford Notch. Visit www.outdoors.org for information and schedules.

Many people attempt to hike in the Presidential Range without proper footgear, clothing, food and water, maps, and other necessities. Some believe that their cell phones will bring immediate rescue should they become lost or injured. This is a mistaken and irresponsible assumption. New Hampshire state law holds hikers liable for the costs of a rescue. If you follow Thoreau in this range, prepare sensibly and walk carefully, and you will enjoy the mountain walk of a lifetime.

2. Mount Greylock

The actual objects which one person will see from a particular hilltop are just as different from those which another will see as the persons are different. The scarlet oak must, in a sense, be in your eye when you go forth. We cannot see anything until we are possessed with the idea of it, and then we can hardly see anything else. . . . This is the history of my finding a score or more of rare plants which I could name.

—JOURNAL, NOVEMBER 4, 1858

Henry David Thoreau had been afield both near his home and to the highest mountains in New England before he turned to the greatest elevation in his home state, Mount Greylock. He came to the 3,491-foot mountain toward the end of a circuitous walk that took him first over Grand Monadnock (see chapters 5 and 12) and then over 2,173-foot Whitcomb Summit in the Hoosac Range. He came down from the Hoosacs into North Adams at the end of July 1844, provisioned himself, and set out for Greylock, or Saddleback, as it was sometimes called. He noted, "I had come over on foot and alone in serene summer days, plucking the raspberries by the wayside, and occasionally buying a loaf of bread at a farmer's house, with a knapsack on my back."

Why Thoreau waited so long in his sauntering career to explore Greylock remains a mystery, but he turned to it enthusiastically on this long tramp into New Hampshire, western Massachusetts, and eastern New York. From North Adams he walked seven miles to the northern end of Greylock's range and tackled the rise through the long ravine that today carries the Bellows Pipe Trail. When Thoreau came here, the route initially followed a cart road that rose in the ravine and connected with mountain farms. This same route today eventually narrows as it ascends, becoming more typically a path at higher elevations.

"I began in the afternoon to ascend the mountain up a long and spacious valley called the Bellows, because the winds rush up or down it with violence in storms, sloping to the very clouds between the principal range and a lower mountain," Thoreau wrote. He would continue south up this ravine, bushwhacking to the summit on a route of his own devising near the top. He camped out on the big mountain's summit, roughing it, and then continued south, meeting his friend William Ellery Channing in Pittsfield. The two eventually returning to Concord after a walk in New York's Catskills.

MOUNT GREYLOCK
ROUTE DESCRIPTION

The Bellows Pipe Trail begins above the junction of Notch and Reservoir Roads south of North Adams. Both roads depart from MA 2 in the Braytonville section of North Adams (watch for a very small sign indicating Greylock Reservation on MA 2) and come together about 1.5 miles farther south near Notch Reservoir. Continuing south, you will find the trailhead on a sharp bend where the mountain's auto road begins at a sharp right turn. The trailhead is marked. There is a small, sometimes muddy parking area there, but better parking is available a short distance just uphill on the auto road.

The trail enters closely grown hardwoods and climbs south over gentle grades on a gravel right-of-way above a brook that feeds Notch Reservoir. This country was largely in pasture or crops when Thoreau arrived here in 1844. The vale was sparsely settled with hill farms, and Thoreau found it inviting enough to remark, "It seemed a good road for the pilgrim to enter upon who would climb to the gates of heaven." He found both the terrain and the settlement interesting. "A stream ran down the middle of the valley, on which near the head there was a mill. . . . Now I crossed a hayfield, and now over the brook on a slight bridge, still gradually ascending all the while, with a sort of awe, and filled with indefinite expectations as to what kind of inhabitants and what kind of nature I should come to at last." Even today you can find scattered remnants of those farms situated here during Thoreau's era.

The trail heads uphill, passes Notch Reservoir to the left and below, and then slabs along the east sides of Mount Williams and

Bellows Pipe Trail

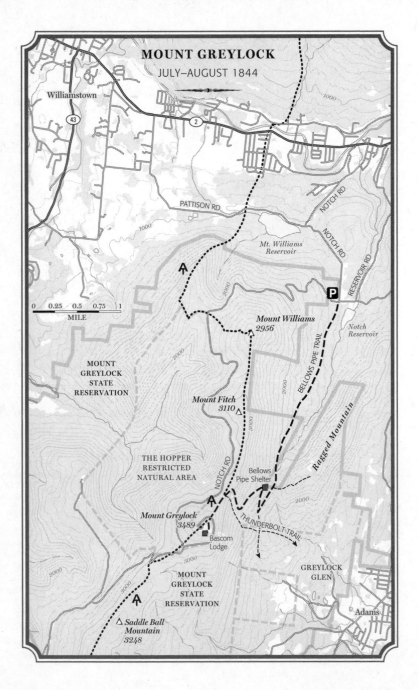

MOUNT GREYLOCK
JULY–AUGUST 1844

Mount Fitch, two lower peaks in the Greylock chain. It crosses several feeder brooks in mostly deciduous growth as it climbs to the south. At 2.2 miles from Notch Road the grade eases slightly at a junction with a side trail on the left to adjacent Ragged Mountain. Thoreau moved toward Ragged a short distance to get a compass bearing on the most direct route to Greylock's summit. He noted of the last farm he passed, "It now seemed some advantage that the earth was uneven, for one could not imagine a more noble position for a farm house than this vale afforded, further from or near to its head, from a glen-like seclusion overlooking the country at a great elevation between these two mountain walls." He prepared to leave the path he had been following as the trail pulled west and determined to "find my own route up the steep, as the shorter and more adventurous way." Relying on the compass bearing he had taken, he "at once entered the woods, and began to climb the steep side of the mountain in a diagonal direction, taking bearing of a tree every dozen rods."

Wherever Thoreau hiked, he routinely ignored warnings from locals that a direct line of ascent was daunting or impossible. He had received, for example, similar admonitions on ascents of Grand Monadnock. He mused upon the fact that the local people he met near many mountains often were not knowledgeable about their own immediate surroundings. "I made my way steadily upward in a straight line," he wrote of Greylock, "through a dense undergrowth of mountain laurel, until the trees began to have a scraggly and infernal look, as if contending with frost goblins, and at length I reached the summit." Here, off-trail, he found that "the ascent was by no means difficult or unpleasant, and occupied much less time than it would have taken to follow the path."

For those content to climb on established routes, the Bellows

Pipe Trail continues upward through black spruce, pine, and low birch cover. The path navigates a substantial depression and then, climbing steadily, reaches the Bellows Pipe Shelter at 2.5 miles. Shortly it turns right (northwest) as the grade grows more challenging, following remnants of an old tote road that winds upward. The trail soon pulls around to the southwest and west while ascending on switchbacks for another half mile to the ridgeline. Views open up here. Junctions with the Appalachian Trail (AT) and, just to the south, the Thunderbolt Trail are reached on the height of land, which offers views to the west.

Turn left (south) on the AT and walk the last 0.3 mile to the summit in low scrub. Cross the auto road and arrive on Greylock's summit, at 5.5 miles. This topmost point, capped by a great stone memorial plinth, is a busy place today, especially in the warm months. Two auto roads allow access to the mountaintop. Greylock is at the center of an 11-mile-long cluster of mountains and offers splendid views over western Massachusetts, eastern New York, and southern Vermont. Ralph Waldo Emerson, who found Greylock to be a demanding hike in 1865 while visiting and lecturing at Williams College, referred to it as "a serious mountain." Dogged by poverty and dreaming of whales, Herman Melville once lived in the valley below to the west.

In Thoreau's time young men from Williams College regularly hiked Greylock and built a makeshift wooden observatory and tower there in 1841. Thoreau spent the night on top, sheltering somewhere in or along the building's open structure. Before turning in, he walked below the summit a short distance to a place where he had spotted a seep. He dug at this spot and created a basin to trap water for drinking, noting that birds were quick to fly to it. Despite the summer season, he found the summit chilly at

Mount Greylock: summit memorial tower

night. He made a windbreak out of boards left around the observatory site, creating, between the windbreak and the single blanket he carried, a sort of unconventional nest for himself that allowed him to sleep.

During the night, the mountain was beset by clouds, only the tower escaping. Thoreau reported, "Once or twice in the night, when I looked up, I saw a white cloud drifting through the windows, and filling the whole upper story." The next morning, he continued, "I was up early and perched on top of this tower to see the daybreak." As it turned out, Thoreau awoke to a sea of clouds. "All around beneath me was spread for a hundred miles on every side, as far as the eye could reach, an undulating country of clouds, answering in the varied swell of its surface to the terrestrial world it veiled."

If you walk around the summit of Greylock on a clear day, you will find views into five states. There are stretches of balsam and red spruce forest on top and wide open spaces surrounding a stone tower. Bascom Lodge, a stone and shingle building dating from Civilian Conservation Corps (CCC) days, offers food and lodging from early June through October. Greylock is actually part of a long ridge, with Mounts Fitch and Williams to the north and Saddle Ball Mountain to the south. The range is protected as Mount Greylock State Reservation, including the Hopper Restricted Natural Area and Greylock Glen. The mountain's substrate is mainly Ordovician phyllite, a metamorphic rock typical of the nearby Taconic Range. Areas of the summit support a boreal, taiga-like cover found only here in Massachusetts. Covered by a layer of ice more than a half mile thick in the Pleistocene, summit ledges show signs of glaciation. Birders come here in season to see 132 avian species, including Bicknell's thrushes and blackpoll warblers. Views of the

local countryside and scattered villages far below are
available on paths around
the summit.

To regain the road and
your starting point, retrace
your steps north on the
AT, bearing right (east) and
downhill on the Bellows
Pipe Trail 0.3 mile north of
Greylock's summit. Descend
carefully on the steep sections below the ridgeline.
Do not attempt to descend
via the Thunderbolt Trail. Be

Interior of Bascom Lodge

sure to stay on the Bellows Pipe Trail, passing the junction with the
side trail to Ragged Mountain's two summits as you hike down
and to the north.

The 11-mile round-trip to the top of Greylock and back to the
trailhead on Notch Road is, for most hikers, a challenging, full-day
activity. Rain and wind gear should be carried even in summer,
along with food and water. It is interesting to recall that on the day
Thoreau hiked here, he covered a total of 16 miles, going over
one range, walking cross-country, and then climbing Greylock. On
the following day, after concluding his exploration of the summit,
he walked another 16 or 17 miles south along the ridge that now
carries the AT and met his friend Channing in Pittsfield, Massachusetts, after which the two hikers undertook a perambulation
through New York's Catskills.

3. Katahdin

It is a faery land where we live—you may walk
out in any direction over the earth's surface—
lifting your horizon—and every where your
path—climbing the convexity of the globe
leads you between heaven and earth—not
away from the light of the sun & stars—& the
habitations of men. I wonder that I get even 5
miles on my way—the walk is so crowded with
events—& phenomena.

—*JOURNAL*, JUNE 7, 1851

O f all the journeys Thoreau made to remote high
places, his 1846 attempt on Maine's Mount
Katahdin deserves to be recognized as an expedition.
In Thoreau's time the mountain lay beyond all settlement, unconnected to anything approaching a road
and reachable mainly via a network of streams and
interconnected lakes. The route lay well beyond the
last lumber camp, far north of any large settlement.
To reach Katahdin's base required a journey from the

Katahdin and some of its multiple summits

Aaron Priest Photography/Shutterstock.com

south of a week or more. The difficulty of such an expedition is unlikely to be overestimated. Poling rapids, making difficult portages, carrying provisions, and maintaining an intact bateau were all constant challenges. And then there was the greater challenge of climbing Katahdin itself.

The 5,271-foot mountain, Maine's loftiest and one of New England's highest, is a giant, rangy massif surrounded by many other elevations northwest of Millinocket. In the interstices, Katahdin looks down on thousands of acres of dense forest and deadwaters, numerous patches of blowdown, and dozens of hid-

den lakes and watercourses. The mountain is now part of Baxter State Park, created out of extensive landholdings donated by former Maine governor Percival Baxter. Being subject to severe weather and other hazards, Katahdin is regularly monitored by park rangers, and access to the high peaks is restricted during inclement weather. In winter, access is by permit only, and groups attempting the summits must meet certain criteria regarding equipment and safety.

Topographically, the mountain is a raised tableland punctuated by six major peaks, visible from almost anywhere in

Maine's northernmost territory. Between South Peak and Chimney Peak (Pamola), Katahdin's Knife Edge offers some of the most exposed and challenging hiking in eastern North America. The mountain's Great Basin, on its north side, looks south and west toward two steep, glaciated chimneys, and its North Basin faces the connected Howe Peaks. The western ridge includes the 3,718-foot Owl and, at a distance, the miles-long ridgeline of Barren Mountain. To the northeast and east are the Basin Ponds at over 2,400 feet and, lower down, Sandy Stream Pond, Roaring Brook, and, more distant, 3,118-foot South Turner Mountain. North and west of the Howe Peaks are seemingly unlimited acres of wild country dotted with still more mountains stretching to northernmost Maine and the Canadian border.

Thoreau's long journey to the mountain is a story in itself. He wrote, "On the 31st of August 1846, I left Concord in Massachusetts for Bangor and the back woods of Maine, by way of the railroad and steamboat, intending to accompany a relative of mine engaged in the timber trade in Bangor, as far as a dam on the West Branch of the Penobscot, in which property he was interested. From this place which is about one hundred miles by the river above Bangor, thirty miles from the Houlton military road, and five miles beyond the last log hut, I proposed to make excursions to Mount Ktaadn, the second highest mountain in New England, about thirty miles distant, and to some of the lakes of the Penobscot."

Thoreau sailed on the Bangor packet, joined his cousin George Thatcher in Bangor, and began the long journey north. "The next forenoon, September 1st," he wrote, "I started with my companion in a buggy from Bangor for 'upriver.' . . . We each had a knapsack or bag filled with such clothing and other arti-

The Katahdin plateau from the southwest   drewthehobbit/Shutterstock.com

cles as were indispensable, and my companion carried his gun." The two men crossed the Penobscot on a ferry and passed the Indian settlements there. "The ferry here took us past Indian Island. . . . In 1837 there were three hundred and sixty-two souls left of this tribe [Abenaki or Penobscot]. . . . We landed in Milford and rode along the east side of the Penobscot, having a more or less constant view of the Penobscot and the Indian islands in it, for they retain all the islands as far up as Nicatow, at the mouth of the East Branch."

The men continued their horse-and-cart travel along one of the few rights-of-way that led to the north. Thoreau commented, "It was the Houlton Road on which we were now traveling. . . . It is the main, almost the only, road in these parts. . . . We crossed the Sunkhaze, a summery Indian name, the Olemon, Passadumkeag, and other streams, which make a greater show on the map than they now did on the road." The two soon found themselves in densely forested, scarcely settled country, the look of which Thoreau found much to his liking. "The beauty of the road itself was remarkable," he wrote. "The various evergreens, many of which are rare with us—delicate and beautiful specimens of the larch, arbor vitae, ball spruce, and fir-balsam from a few inches to many feet in height, lined its sides, in some places like a long front yard, springing up from the smooth grass plots which uninterruptedly border it. . . . While it was but a step on either hand to the grim untrodden wilderness, whose tangled labyrinth of living, fallen and decaying trees—only the deer and moose, the bear and the wolf, can easily penetrate."

The Penobscot divided, and Thoreau and his cousin turned up the West Branch. Having left their horse and cart behind, they commenced a further walk northwest. "Leaping over a fence," Thoreau recorded, "we began to follow an obscure trail up the northern bank of the Penobscot. There was now no road further—the river being the only highway." As they hunted for the trail, Thoreau observed, "We found the East Branch a large and rapid stream at its mouth, and much deeper than it appeared. Having with some difficulty discovered the trail again, we kept up the south side of the West Branch, or main river, passing by some of the rapids called rock-ebeeme, the roar of which we heard through the woods."

The remoteness of their situation deepened as they arrived at an outpost known as Waite's Farm, which Thoreau described as "an extensive and elevated clearing from which we got a fine view of the river, rippling and gleaming far beneath us. . . . We could overlook an immense country of uninterrupted forest stretching way up the East Branch toward Canada, on the north and northwest, and toward the Aroostook Valley on the northeast, and imagine what wild life was stirring in its midst."

Thoreau and Thatcher arranged with George McCauslin to guide them upriver when the Indian guides they had hired failed to appear. McCauslin had the reputation of being the area's most adept riverman, an estimate fully borne out as he and his son poled Thoreau and Thatcher up through the rapids in a traditional bateau. Of a cabin site called Old Fowler's, Thoreau remarked, "Here our new bateau was to be carried over the first portage of two miles, round the grand falls of the Penobscot." And as they grew nearer Katahdin, he wrote, "We were soon in the smooth waters of Quakish Lake and took our turns at rowing and paddling across it. . . . We had our first but partial view of Ktaadn, its summit veiled in clouds, like a dark isthmus in that quarter, connecting the heavens with the earth."

> *"We had our first but partial view of Ktaadn, its summit veiled in clouds, like a dark isthmus in that quarter, connecting the heavens with the earth."*

Thoreau thought they were "about 30 miles by the river from the summit of Ktaadn, which was in sight, though not more than twenty in a straight line." At this point he believed they had come about a hundred miles north of Bangor. They continued on, finding their way through the tangle of lakes, which they would probably have been unable to do without McCauslin. Each time the stream they were on entered a lake, it was extremely difficult to find the exit, leading into another stream and thence onward. Thoreau noted, "After poling up half a mile of river, or thoroughfare, we rowed a mile across the foot of Pamadumcook Lake, which is the name given on the map to this whole chain of lakes, as if there was but one." Shortly, they navigated into Deep Cove and then into Ambejijis Lake. Said Thoreau, "Ambejijis, this quiet Sunday morning, struck me as the most beautiful lake we had seen. It is said to be one of the deepest. We had the fairest view of Jo-Merry, Doubletop and Ktaadn, from its surface. The summit of the latter had a singularly flat table-land appearance, like a short highway where a demi-god might be let down to take a turn or two in an afternoon to settle his dinner."

Thoreau and his party made another portage and found themselves next in the Nesowadnehunk Deadwater and then Aboljacknagesic Stream. Their journey was nearly over. Now they were in the shadow of the mountain. All that remained was to climb it. Thoreau's attempt on the mountain was certainly not the first. Katahdin was probably first climbed by whites in 1804. A path of sorts, known as the Abol slide route, rose steeply from what is now Abol Campground. There also may have been a crude route up the long ridgeline on the mountain's western flank where today the Hunt Trail rises. But none of this mattered. Thoreau was about to proceed in a manner that he often preferred. He would lead his party on a bushwhack up Katahdin, avoiding whatever established routes might be available to him.

After resting for the night, the group got ready to ascend early the next day. "By six o'clock," Thoreau wrote, "having mounted our packs and a good blanket full of trout, ready dressed, and swung up such baggage and provision as we wished to leave behind upon the tops of saplings, to be out of reach of bears, we started for the mountain, distant as Uncle George and the boatmen called it, about four miles, but as I judged, and as it proved, nearer fourteen. He had never been any nearer to the mountain than this, and there was not the slightest trace of man to guide us further in this direction. . . . Here it fell to my lot, as the oldest mountain climber, to take the lead: so scanning the woody side of the mountain, which lay still at an indefinite distance, stretched out some seven or eight miles in length in front of us, we determined to steer directly for the base of the highest peak, leaving a large slide by which, as I have since learned, some of our predecessors ascended, on our left."

Thoreau's penchant for finding his own route, for bushwhacking across country, motivated him in some way to ignore other possibilities for the ascent. His comments indicate that he may not have fully understood that the Abol slide route was the most direct path to Katahdin's main summit until later, despite knowing someone who had climbed the slide route before.

He continued, "This course would lead us parallel to a dark seam in the forest, which marked the bed of a torrent, and over a slight spur, which extended southward from the main mountain, from whose bare summit we could get an outlook over the country, and climb directly up the peak, which would then be close at hand. . . . Setting the compass for a northeast course, which was the bearing of the southern base of the highest peak we were soon buried in the woods." The choice of this route to Katahdin's South Peak would present a serious complication, as Thoreau soon learned.

The party moved up the densely wooded slopes of 3,400-foot Rum Mountain, which lay about a mile south of Katahdin's summit ridge. Thoreau described their progress, noting, "We had proceeded thus seven or eight miles, till about noon, with frequent pauses to refresh the weary ones, crossing a considerable mountain stream, which we conjectured to be Murch Brook [actually Abol Stream], at whose mouth we had camped, all the time in the woods, without once having seen the summit. . . . By the side of a cool mountain rill, amid the woods, where the water began to partake of the purity and the transparency of air, we stopped to cook some of our fishes."

> *"By the side of a cool mountain rill, amid the woods, where the water began to partake of the purity and the transparency of air, we stopped to cook some of our fishes."*

After lunching on blueberries as he climbed, Thoreau seems to have become less sure that this was the best route. It was September 7 now, and he wrote, "At length, fearing that if we held the direct course to the summit, we should not find any water near our camping ground, we gradually swerved to the west, till, at four o'clock, we struck again the torrent which I have mentioned, and here, in view of the summit, the weary party decided to camp that night."

Thoreau's cohorts set up camp in a "deep and narrow ravine, sloping up to the clouds, at an angle of nearly forty-five degrees, and hemmed in by walls of rock, which were at first covered by low trees, then impenetrable thickets of scraggly birches and spruce trees, and with moss, but at last bare of all vegetation but lichens, and almost continually draped in clouds." He decided to continue upward alone a ways before sunset.

Thoreau's decision to bushwhack his way to the summit now forced him to clamber up the steep streambed, the only clear opening, using handholds to pull himself up. Short of technical climbing, it was the most physically demanding means of getting up Katahdin. He, having advanced in the stream's flow, and his gear were soaking wet. "Following up the course of the torrent which occupied this—and I mean to lay some emphasis on this word up—pulling myself up by the side of perpendicular falls of twenty or thirty feet, by the roots of firs and birches, and then, perhaps, walking a level rod or two in the thin stream, for it took up the whole road, ascending by huge steps, as if it were a giant's stairway, down which a river flowed, I had soon cleared the trees and paused on the successive shelves, to look back over the country."

He later remembered, "The torrent was from fifteen to thirty feet wide, without a tributary, and seemingly not diminishing in breadth as I advanced; but still it came rushing and roaring down, with a copious tide, over and amidst masses of bare rock, from the very clouds, as though a water-spout had just burst over the mountain. Leaving this at last, I began to work my way, scarcely less arduous than Satan's anciently through Chaos, up the nearest, though not the highest peak."

With a change in direction, Thoreau was now heading for Baxter Peak rather than South Peak, which had been his earlier choice. (He had, it seems, mistakenly believed South Peak to be the loftier of the two.) Of Katahdin's many peaks, Baxter is the highest, at 5,271 feet. Having scrambled out of the upper limits of Abol Stream, he now had more climbing to do.

"At first scrambling on all fours over the tops of ancient black spruce-trees *(Albes nigra),* old as the flood, from two to ten or twelve feet in height, their tops flat and spreading, and their foliage blue and nipt with cold, as if for centuries they had ceased growing upward against the bleak sky, the solid cold. I walked some good rods erect upon the tops of these trees, which were overgrown with moss and mountain-cranberries. It seemed that in the course of time they had filled up the intervals between the huge rocks, and the cold wind had uniformly levelled all over."

Making his way over the krummholz, Thoreau was in danger of a fall or other injury. "Once, slumping through, I looked down ten feet into a dark and cavernous region, and saw the stem of a spruce, on whose top I stood, as on a mass of coarse basket-work, fully nine inches in diameter at the ground. These holes were bear's dens, and the bears were even then at home." Krummholz, essentially conifers growing horizontally in a tangled, dense, impenetrable net to resist wind, cannot be walked through but may sometimes support a person trying to make his or her way over these barriers. One can just as well fall through these tangles and be injured.

Thoreau continued, "This

> *"At first scrambling on all fours over the tops of ancient black spruce-trees* (Albes nigra), *old as the flood, from two to ten or twelve feet in height, their tops flat and spreading, and their foliage blue and nipt with cold, as if for centuries they had ceased growing upward against the bleak sky, the solid cold.*

was the sort of garden I made my way over for an eighth of a mile, at the risk, it is true, of treading on some of the plants, not seeing any path through it—certainly the most treacherous and porous country I ever travelled. . . . Having slumped, scrambled, rolled, bounced, and walked, by turns, over this scraggy country, I arrived upon a side hill or rather side mountain, where rocks, gray, silent rocks, were the flocks and herds that pastured, chewing a rocky cud at sunset. . . . This brought me to the skirt of a cloud, and bounded my walk that night."

Some argument exists as to just how far Thoreau went as he emerged on Katahdin's summit plateau, or if he arrived there at all. With dark coming on and the heights swept by clouds, he descended to the party's provisional campsite, a place that he described as "a savage and dreary scenery enough, so wildly rough." The next morning the whole party began the ascent, with Thoreau again in the lead. He soon outpaced them and disappeared into the clouds above, which opened and closed in the wind. He wrote, "Now the wind would blow me out a yard of clear sunlight wherein I stood; then a gray, dawning light was all it could accomplish, the cloud-line ever rising and falling with the wind's intensity." Wherever he stood, nearby but not on either of the two closest peaks, he caught random views of his surroundings and then prepared to go down once more. "Fearing that my companions would be anxious to reach the river before night, and knowing that the clouds might rest on the mountain for days, I was compelled to descend." When he reached them, his companions were still busy collecting mountain cranberries and blueberries. He noted, "From this elevation, just on the skirts of the clouds, we could overlook the country west and south for a hundred miles. There it was, the state of

Maine, which we had seen on the map, but not much like that,—immeasurable forest for the sun to shine on, that eastern stuff we hear of in Massachusetts. No clearing, no house. It does not look as if a solitary traveler had cut so much as a walking stick there."

Trying to lead the party back to lower ground and the place where they had left their bateau, McCauslin climbed a tree to determine their course. He took a bearing on "a little meadow and a pond," toward which they then walked. "Pursuing this course," Thoreau wrote, "we soon reached the open land, which went sloping down some miles toward the Penobscot." He was deeply affected by how remote this country was, how wild its character, as he made his way back to the river. "Perhaps I most fully realized that this was primeval, untamed, and forever un-tameable Nature, or whatever else men call it, while coming down this part of the mountain. . . . Nature was here something savage and awful, though beautiful. . . . Here was no man's garden, but the unhandselled globe."

KATAHDIN
ROUTE DESCRIPTION

Hikers wishing to replicate Thoreau's 1846 climb should be suitably prepared and well equipped. The shortest route to Baxter Peak along the Abol Trail, nearly the same route Thoreau used, offers challenges suitable for fit, experienced hikers used to big-mountain tramping. The Abol Trail requires nearly 4,000 feet of elevation gain during the 3.8-mile ascent on it and the connecting

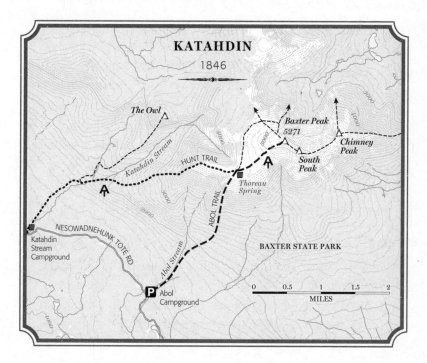

Hunt Trail to Katahdin's highest summit. Until the mountain's upper plateau is reached, grades are steep and continuous. The descent from Baxter Peak on the Abol Trail is no less demanding, traveling over loose scree and through boulder fields, and with nearly continuous exposure to the elements.

On Katahdin it is essential to wear good-quality hiking boots with lug soles and to carry a pack with foul-weather clothing, a sweater or fleece jacket for warmth, a hat and gloves, and plenty of water and food. You should always carry a map and compass, and you should know how to use them. If you wish to camp in Baxter, before or after making an ascent, you must make reservations online with the park authority (www.baxterstateparkauthority .com/reservation/) and pay a fee.

"Nature was here something savage and awful, though beautiful. . . . Here was no man's garden, but the unhandselled globe."

The Abol Trail climbs the outwash of a substantial mountain slide that occurred in 1816. A subsequent smaller slide also occurred, and some minor movement of materials is to be expected with human presence and weathering. The Appalachian Mountain Club warns that this hike is potentially dangerous because of the route's steep terrain and loose footing. Park rangers may close this or other Baxter State Park trails when weather poses a threat. Accidental injury on Katahdin is especially worrisome, as the mountain lies a long way from hospital-level emergency care. If injury occurs, evacuation is very difficult and sometimes impossible. You are responsible for your own safety.

Baxter State Park is reached from I-95 via Millinocket. The great mountain can be seen, looming to the west, from many points on the highway. Once in the park, follow the Nesowadne-hunk Tote Road northwest to Abol Campground. From the tenting area, which is located on what was probably an aboriginal site, walk northeast on the Abol Trail and then onto an old carry road, which shortly parallels a feeder brook to Abol Stream. About 0.75 mile above the campground the path pulls away from the stream, going abruptly right (northeast). Soon established old-growth vegetation gives way to the new, largely deciduous forest that has sprung up on the slide's outwash over the years. Grades are moderate here.

Shortly the trail heads directly up the slide, pulling away from the brook and threading its way through the gravel and rocky debris that have fallen here. In most places the footing is firm, but occasionally it is soft, giving way. Use caution. As the last vegetation is passed, good views to the south, southeast, and southwest gradually open up. Thoreau's route lay to the east a short distance. As he climbed, he walked directly in the Abol streambed, contending, as I have described, with the daunting tangled growth and boulder tumble that bordered his chosen line of ascent. Katahdin historian John Neff believes the Abol slide route was the one used by the mountain's earliest explorers. Neff says that the first known ascent of this slide was made in 1819 by Colin Campbell and a team of British explorers, who built a small shelter on a shelf above. A succession of camps were constructed here, culminating in a log hut built by fire warden Frank Sewall between 1913 and 1917. At just under 2 miles, the path climbs more steeply through evidence of later slide activity and then into an open boulder field. Thoreau saw similar terrain a few hundred yards to the east, emerging twice into heavy clouds and leaving the mountain without summiting.

Above the most demanding section, the Abol Trail eases, crossing a plateau briefly to arrive at Thoreau Spring at 4,627 feet. Here you turn right (east), following the Hunt Trail along the height of land on more moderate grades, soon arriving at the mountain's highest point, 5,271-foot Baxter Peak. From this bare, rocky summit, the official northern terminus of the Appalachian Trail, there are splendid views in all directions. You'll be glad you brought your camera and binoculars.

I recommend using a map and a compass to identify the many mountains and bodies of water that surround Katahdin. "The Complete Map of Mt. Katahdin and Baxter State Park," issued by Maine Guide James Witherell, is useful because of its topographical information. (You can find this map in stores in Millinocket and Bangor, in bookstores, and at outfitters such as L.L.Bean and EMS.)

Chimney Pond Camp as it once was   Maine State Museum Collections

Also helpful is the AMC's "Maine Mountains Trail Map," Baxter State Park–Katahdin sheet, which shows all trails currently open in the area.

To descend, retrace your steps with great care down the Hunt and Abol Trails. Leave Baxter Peak in plenty of time to get down before dark. Do not attempt "shortcuts" or other deviations from the trails. Visitors who have attempted to make their way off-trail have suffered injuries and even death (see Donn Fendler's *Lost on a Mountain in Maine*). You can also follow the Hunt Trail all the way down to Katahdin Stream Campground, turn left (east) on the Nesowadnehunk Tote Road, and walk back to your starting point at Abol Stream. An ascent up the Abol and Hunt Trails with a descent westward via the Hunt Trail, including the walk back along the road to Abol Stream, is roughly 10 miles and takes nearly 8 hours. The same ascent with a descent via the Hunt and Abol Trails is about 7.6 miles and takes 7 hours.

4. Pack Monadnock
IN THE WAPACK RANGE

I trust that the walkers of the present day are conscious of the blessings which they enjoy in the comparative freedom with which they can ramble over the country & enjoy the landscape—anticipating with compassion that future day when possibly it will be partitioned off into so called pleasure grounds where only a few may enjoy the narrow and exclusive pleasure which is compatible with ownership. . . . I am thankfull that we have yet so much room in America.

—*JOURNAL*, FEBRUARY 12, 1851

Southwestern New Hampshire is hill country, an area beautifully dotted with dozens of small mountains around its famous regional centerpiece, Grand Monadnock. Henry David Thoreau first traveled here in 1844, continuing on to Whitcomb

> *"It is pleasant thus to look from afar into winter. We look at a condition which we have not reached. Notwithstanding the poverty of the immediate landscape, in the horizon it is simplicity and grandeur."*

Summit in the Hoosac Range in Massachusetts. Thoreau didn't write at length about his first trip to the region, during which he spent two or three days exploring Grand Monadnock. Some have speculated about the routes he walked on the mountain, but we do not know exactly where he climbed during this early visit. What seems certain is that he developed an affection for the area, the mountain, and its surroundings, returning periodically to hike and camp here. These later excursions drew comment in Thoreau's extensive journals, and it is to the earliest of these recorded trips that we turn now.

Thoreau kept an eye on the mountains he could see from those bits of higher ground around Concord that he walked regularly. Winter and summer, he looked west to elevations such as Wachusett Mountain in Massachusetts and Grand Monadnock and the other mountains around it in New Hampshire. In November of 1851 he remarked, "I can see snow on the Peterboro hills, reflecting the sun. It is pleasant thus to look from afar into winter. We look at a condition which we have not reached. Notwithstanding the poverty of the immediate landscape, in the horizon it is simplicity and grandeur. I look into valleys white with snow and now lit up by the sun, while all the country is in shade."

Just east of Grand Monadnock lies the Wapack Range, a

collection of lower summits that begins in western Massachusetts and crosses into New Hampshire, running north to North Pack Monadnock in Greenfield. These are the hills that Thoreau viewed in winter. He returned to this region in September of 1852, hiking first in the Wapack Range and then heading west to ascend Grand Monadnock again. Arriving by railroad at what is now Greenville on September 6, Thoreau walked north to Temple, then bushwhacked over an arm of Temple Mountain and, later, to the summit of Pack Monadnock. From there he descended west to Peterborough, where he rested for the night.

The next day, September 7, he arose early, as he preferred, and walked roughly seven miles cross-country to some point near the northeast side of Grand Monadnock, climbing the 3,165-foot mountain along a route of his own devising. Thoreau did not tarry long on the summit, but descended the southwest side of the great mountain rapidly in the afternoon, going directly to the railroad station in Troy. By my calculation, he had walked more than twenty miles on September 6 and 7, including crossing the two highest summits in the region. As you can see, we will have some work to do to keep up with him.

PACK MONADNOCK
ROUTE DESCRIPTION

———◆———

Begin at the point where the Wapack Trail crosses NH 101 at Miller State Park, just under 3 miles east of NH 101's junction with NH 123 and 2 miles west of its intersection with NH 45. Cars may be left here for day hiking or overnight trips. Camping is not permitted.

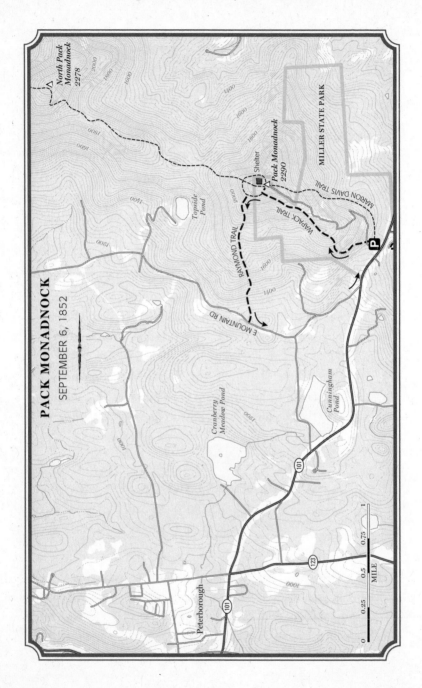

PACK MONADNOCK

SEPTEMBER 6, 1852

North Pack
Monadnock
2278

Topside
Pond

Shelter

Pack Monadnock
2290

MILLER STATE PARK

MARION DAVIS TRAIL

WAPACK TRAIL

RAYMOND TRAIL

E MOUNTAIN RD

Cranberry
Meadow Pond

Cunningham
Pond

Peterborough

101

101

123

MILE

0   0.25   0.5   0.75   1

The trailhead lies at the north-east corner of the parking lot by a trail board.

As mentioned, Thoreau came to this place after hiking northwest cross-country from Temple village, hoping to reach high ground where he could see Grand Monadnock. He appears to have ascended 1,600-foot Whitcomb Peak, on Temple Mountain's east flank. Still not being able to spy Grand Monadnock, he descended to the location

Trail junction, Pack Monadnock summit

described above, with a view to continuing northward. Walking over Whitcomb Peak, he observed, "We went down the west side of this first mountain, from whose summit we could not see west on account of another ridge [Temple Mountain]; descended far, and across the road, and up the southernmost of what I have called the Peterboro Hills." (Thoreau used this term to refer to Pack Monadnock and North Pack Monadnock.)

From the parking lot, the Wapack Trail ascends left (north) at the junction with the blue-blazed Marion Davis Trail. Follow the Wapack Trail across the mountain's auto road, then clamber over a rough boulder field under hanging cliffs. Proceed under the power lines and up the steeper ledges that lie ahead to the north-west. This is varied terrain, as the trail gains and loses elevation here. It then veers abruptly right and again runs to the northwest, climbing steadily through mixed growth.

Shortly the trail passes through several birch-lined openings with views west to Grand Monadnock and, behind it, some lower Vermont hills. Though the trail is forested now, mostly open ground greeted Thoreau as he ascended here. Hill farms were common along the Wapack Range, and much of this terrain was formerly cleared for pasture. Numerous stretches of old, high pasture and abandoned orchards remain along the trail today. Old stone walls wander the mountain all the way up to the summit in places. As the trail reaches the ridgeline, the grade eases, with occasional narrow views west to Cranberry Meadow Pond and Cunningham Pond as it continues north-northeast. Lowbush blueberry and ground juniper cover islands of open ledge amid stands of wiry red oak.

Descending into denser woods, the trail runs through a low wet area 1 mile above the trailhead. It proceeds through a stand of dense black spruce that continues for about a quarter mile. Wood sorrel and mountain ash occasionally interrupt the spruce cover. Of his march up Pack Monadnock, Thoreau remembered stands of "glaringly white" birches and observed, "There is something in the aspect of the evergreens, the dwarfed forests, and the bare rocks of mountaintops, and the scent of ferns, stern yet sweet to man."

The trail slabs along the west face of the mountain, just below the highest point of the ridge here. A fine stand of hemlock graces the trail as it nears the top. Follow the trail to the right and upward, to the southeast, then onto the auto road. The road was established here by the Civilian Conservation Corps (CCC) in 1936. Yellow triangles on the road guide you to a right fork, where you pass the Marion Davis Trail on the right, then arrive in a few steps on the 2,290-foot summit. There are views here over Temple Moun-

Summit of Pack Monadnock

tain to the south. The short Red Circle Trail provides a pleasant around-the-summit walk of less than half a mile, offering further excellent views, including those toward the imposing mass of Grand Monadnock just to the west. An observation tower offers additional outlooks.

If the summit is busy when you arrive, look for a "Wapack" sign by a stone shelter on the north side of the road and descend northward just 0.1 mile to a level, ledgy area, where you can rest and perhaps have lunch. New Hampshire Audubon conducts a hawk census here each September and October. On a recent cold, windy autumn day here, I discovered that observers had tallied several thousand buteos and accipiters during the two-month period. At this spot, Thoreau would have seen his route of the

New Hampshire Audubon hawk monitoring station

following day, a more or less straight line cross-country to Grand Monadnock to the west. And he might have assessed the countryside through which he was making his way, delighting in its pleasant assault on his senses. As he wrote in his notable essay on walking, "In my walks I would fain return to my senses. What business have I in the woods, if I am thinking of something out of the woods? . . . An absolutely new prospect is a great happiness, and I can still get this any afternoon."

Thoreau continued on a short distance toward North Pack Monadnock from here, then left the trail and descended to the northwest, passing Topside Pond and continuing on local roads into Peterborough. From the summit of Pack Monadnock, you have three choices of descent. First, you can simply retrace your earlier route down to the Miller State Park parking lot. Second, you can continue west down the interesting Raymond Trail to East Moun-

View to the northwest from Pack Monadnock

tain Road in Peterborough, then walk south along the road about 1.25 miles to your starting point. Finally, you can descend via the Marion Davis Trail, a route that slabs along the eastern slope of the mountain to the Miller State Park lot.

I recommend descending via the Raymond Trail, as it most closely approximates Thoreau's descent and runs through attractive woods away from the auto road. Leave the Wapack Trail at its junction with the white-arrow-blazed Raymond Trail (sign), cross the Red Circle Trail, and hike down over ledge, shortly reaching a series of stone steps dropping west. The grade is steep for a few hundred yards, interrupted by several shelves where the terrain levels off. Thoreau's descent from the summit paralleled this trail just a short distance to the north as he headed for Peterborough center.

About a quarter mile below the ridgeline, the trail enters two

Summit tower, Pack Monadnock

or three open spaces with good views to the west. Here you see essentially what Thoreau might have seen, except for the few intrusions of modernity. The trail then descends steeply over a rockfall and onto a plateau, turning left (south). Soon it pulls westward again, and just under 1 mile below the summit it passes a short side trail to a brook and then drops into a depression, crossing a second brook in deciduous forest. The path continues through a stone wall, drops to a low ridge, and then rises slightly to the northwest, arriving at East Mountain Road 1.5 miles below Pack Monadnock's highest point. Turn left (south) on the road and follow it to the Miller State Park parking lot.

Note: On the summit of Pack Monadnock drinking water is available at the warden's cabin in the milder months, and there are primitive toilets just north of the cabin site. The auto road is open only from late spring through autumn. Use caution when crossing or walking along the road. Please leave no trace of your passing.

5. Grand Monadnock

(EAST)

My desire for knowledge is intermittent but
my desire to commune with the spirits of the
universe—to be intoxicated even with the
fumes, call it, of that divine nectar—to bear
my head through atmospheres and over
heights unknown to my feet—is perennial and
constant.

—*JOURNAL*, FEBRUARY 9, 1851

Following an exploratory hike over Temple
Mountain's eastern arm and then to the summit
of Pack Monadnock, Thoreau spent the night of September 6, 1852, in Peterborough, New Hampshire.
With William Ellery Channing, he had covered
around fifteen miles that day over what was, for both
men, new territory and the region's second-highest
rise. They had walked from Mason Station to Temple,
over high ground in the Wapack Range, and then on

to Peterborough. This, as it proved, was a mere warm-up for Thoreau.

On the morning of September 7 he was primed to make his second hike over nearby 3,159-foot Grand Monadnock. He had climbed the mountain for the first time in July of 1844, though it isn't clear where exactly he hiked then. Now, as part of this journey, he would include another, if unusually hurried, visit to the summit. Grand Monadnock was a mountain that he would keep coming back to and that he would examine with great enthusiasm.

Generally when Thoreau chose to explore, he would move about slowly and observe with great patience the details of his natural surroundings. At such moments his movements were often both celebratory and reverent. His vast output as a writer confirms this repeatedly. But on this day Thoreau was quite another fellow. He was not prepared to tarry. He was instead eager to transit the larger mountain, to inspect its highest points once again, and to be home by dinner. His ability to move rapidly when he desired served him perfectly for this day's effort. He had no time to waste.

This ascent was likely Thoreau's first from Grand Monadnock's east side. As was often the case with his mountaineering, there was a long, vigorous walk before the actual ascent. He and Channing tramped the distance from Peterborough across country, saving themselves a longer stroll than had they followed existing roads. In his journal he wrote that he had walked miles "across lots still, to Monadnock, the base some half-dozen miles in a straight line from Peterboro." Upon his arrival at the foot of Grand Monadnock, he wrote, "my clothes [were] sprinkled with ambrosia pollen." There were better-known and perhaps easier routes to the summit from the southeast, but Thoreau, who was still "learning" the mountain, wanted to find his own way uphill. He and Channing took to the woods near Thorndike Pond, headed for a day's outing on Grand Monadnock's high ledges.

GRAND MONADNOCK (EAST)
ROUTE DESCRIPTION

A network of trails that parallel Thoreau's 1852 bushwhack rises just south of his probable route. By linking four different trails, you can very closely approximate Thoreau's climb, which rose up through a ravine and along a streambed on the east side of the mountain. To find the trailhead, drive north on NH 124 for 3 miles from its junction with NH 137 and US 202 in Jaffrey to Jaffrey Center. Turn right (north) on Dublin Road and continue north past Poole Road to the entrance to Gilson Pond Campground. From NH 101 in Dublin, drive south on Upper Jaffrey Road 3.5 miles to the campground. Parking is available in a hiker's lot beyond the gate. Park maps are available at the gate.

To begin this hike, follow signs for the Pond Loop Trail, which runs southwest off the campground road along the southern shore of Gilson Pond. There are frequent water views from this path, which follows the pond perimeter. Stay with this trail a short distance, walking southwest and west through an area of pine and hemlock to the point where the Pond Loop Trail pulls right (northwest). Bear left here and walk southwest and west on the Birchtoft Trail, which continues toward the mountain on easy grades.

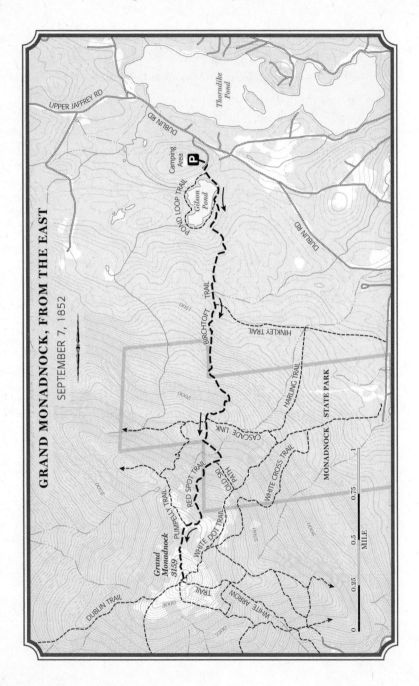

GRAND MONADNOCK, FROM THE EAST
SEPTEMBER 7, 1852

Gilson Pond Campground entrance at Monadnock State Park

Somewhere just north of here, Thoreau headed uphill, spotting "Joe Eavely's, the house nearest the top, that we saw under the east side, a small red house a little way up." He continued past the house and followed Eleveth Brook up the ravine, a route hikers may parallel on the established route described here.

Continue on the Birchtoft Trail as it meanders through mixed-growth woodlands, soon intersecting with two old ski trails and reaching a junction with the Hinkley Trail at just under 1 mile from the trailhead. Thoreau noted on his hike that he "saw bunchberries everywhere now," and he identified a variety of young maples as he walked uphill. Stay on the Birchtoft Trail and begin the rise westward on moderate grades. The pitch gradually steepens as the route drifts southwest and then northwest as the trail nears a junction

Birchtoft Trail

with the Cascade Link in another mile, at the 2,100-foot contour line. Here the Birchtoft Trail ends.

Go straight ahead (west) on the Cascade Link for a short distance. At a junction, leave the Cascade Link and take the Red Spot Trail west. This path, marked with red and white blazes, provides a rough and ready connector that pulls southwest, crosses two seasonal brooks, and then saws its way upward in bends and switchbacks, generally climbing northwest toward the ridge. In a half mile the trail passes the Old Ski Path Trail on the left, and a quarter mile beyond that it emerges on open ledges with increasingly broad views. At about 2,900 feet the Red Spot Trail turns to the north for a couple of hundred yards and reaches the Pumpelly Trail at a T marked by a big cairn.

Turn left (west) on the Pumpelly Trail, following this fine, open ridge walk generally westward. The trail dips into a rocky cleft briefly, then winds up over more open ledge marked by cairns and a series of shallow glacial pans. Along this last 0.4-mile rise to Grand Monadnock's summit are some of the best views from any elevation in southwestern New Hampshire. This section is quite exposed; be careful to stay on the path in cloud cover or precipitation.

Once on top, Thoreau surveyed the vegetation he found scattered about the mountain's metamorphic dome, which is mostly fashioned of layered schist and quartzite. "Between rocks on the summit [was] an abundance of . . . blueberries still . . . very large, fresh, and cooling to eat, supplying the place of water," he wrote. Looking about the summit, he further noted, "Though this vegetation was very humble, yet it was very productive of fruit." And later he observed, "The little soil on the summit between the rocks was covered with the Potentilla tridentata, now out of bloom, the prevailing plant at the extreme summit." He would explore Grand

Trailboard, Mount Monadnock, east side

Monadnock much more thoroughly in 1858 and 1860, camping and botanizing all around the summit and connected plateaus.

During his several visits to the mountain, Thoreau carefully compiled a list of plants, fruits, flowers, shrubs, and trees that he observed in his wanderings. It is likely that he was one of the first individuals to so thoroughly probe Monadnock's natural inheritance. In 2006 Dianne Eno, a graduate student at Antioch University New England, studied the historic and continuing presence of plant taxa on Monadnock. She began with Thoreau's discovery of seventy-six species here. Examining today's distribution of plant species on the mountain, Eno found that 96 percent of the types identified by Thoreau in 1860 and earlier are still present and flourishing on the summit and in forested areas below timberline.

On that September day in 1852, however, Thoreau would not

linger. He and Channing strode rapidly down the mountain's south-west reaches and proceeded, at a run, to the railroad station in Troy, where they caught a train going east to Concord. You can make a more rational and pleasant descent by retracing your steps carefully northeastward on the Pumpelly Trail, being careful to turn right (east) on the Red Spot Trail. Stay with the route you followed earlier, descending east to the trailhead at Gilson Pond via the Red Spot, Birchtoft, and Pond Loop Trails. The round-trip to the summit and back is 6.4 miles. Make sure to carry plenty of water, food, a compass, a flashlight, and appropriate clothing regardless of the time of year. In addition to the map in this book, the Appalachian Mountain Club's "Southern New Hampshire Trail Map," which includes Mount Monadnock, may prove useful when hiking here.

6.
Wachusett Mountain

———◦———

Men nowhere, east or west, live yet a *natural* life, round which the vine clings, and which the elm willingly shadows. Man would desecrate it by his touch, and so the beauty of the world remains veiled to him. He needs not only to be spiritualized, but *naturalized,* on the soil of the earth.

—*A WEEK ON THE CONCORD AND MERRIMACK RIVERS*

The part of Massachusetts that hugs the Atlantic shore is, with the exception of Great Blue Hill south of Boston, a terrain of little elevation. Those Bay Staters interested in mountains, and Henry David Thoreau was certainly one of them, turn their gaze westward. Thoreau often visited local rises around Concord, following his own injunction to "be careful to sit in an elevating and inspiring place." Regularly looking west to central Massachusetts, he was enthralled by the raised blue line that lay nearly thirty miles away: Wachusett Mountain. He even sketched this distant ridgeline in his journal.

Because it was his habit to keep a proprietary eye on Wachusett and other hills to the west and northwest, one might say that he was conscious of these homegrown mountains even when he was busy about Concord. During his local rambles, he made notes on those higher elevations and the surrounding communities. They were, at the very least, often on his mind, and they showed up regularly in his written comments. In his journal he wrote, "In many moods it is cheering to look across hence to that blue rim of the earth, and be reminded of the invisible towns and communities . . . which lie in the further and deeper hollows between me and these hills."

As Thoreau walked the small rises near Concord again and again, his eye took in the Wapack Range and the Monadnock hills in southwestern New Hampshire. And these distant views, as they have been to many who hike and climb, were an inspiration to him. But it was the thin blue line closer to home that held his attention and impelled a journey out from the sedate lanes of his hometown.

Wachusett Mountain is a 2,006-foot peak in Sterling, just south of Westminster. Thoreau at last made his first trip there in July of 1842. His "hike" on Wachusett actually began before 5 AM on July 19 in Concord. There was, you see, the small matter of getting to the mountain. He and Richard Fuller walked cross-country through Acton, Stowe, and Bolton, traversing hop fields and pastures. In a *Boston Miscellany* report of the expedition, Thoreau noted, "Before noon we had reached the highlands overlooking the valley of Lancaster (affording the first fair and open prospect into the west), and there, on the top of a hill, in the shade of some oaks, near to where a spring bubbled out from a leaden pipe, we rested during the heat of a day, reading Virgil and enjoying the scenery." It is worth observing that the two were carrying a heavier load than Thoreau normally required, as their kit included a burdensome two-man tent.

> *"There, on the top of a hill, in the shade of some oaks, near to where a spring bubbled out from a leaden pipe, we rested during the heat of a day, reading Virgil and enjoying the scenery."*

The hikers generally followed the course of the Nashua and Stillwater Rivers and picked raspberries along the road. Later Thoreau wrote, "Fifteen miles further to the west, beyond the deep and broad valley in which lie Groton, Shirley, Lancaster, and Boylston, runs the Wachusett range, in the same general direction." After walking at least twenty-five miles that day, they took lodging that evening in West Sterling, four miles from their intended goal.

On this first visit to Wachusett, Thoreau ascended the mountain on its north side, on or near what are now the Bolton Pond and Old Indian Trails. These trails are today intersected by ski slopes on the mountain's northeast flank. Thoreau and Fuller carried the cumbersome tent up to the summit, where they established camp. Thoreau described the summit as a dome of bare rock punctuated by blueberry, gooseberry, and strawberry, with stands of "a fine, wiry grass." He wrote, "Before sunset, we rambled along the ridge to the north, while a hawk soared still above us."

Of the overnight stay, Thoreau noted, "It was thrilling to hear the wind roar over the rocks, at intervals when we waked, for it had grown quite cold and windy. The night was, in its elements, simple even to majesty in that bleak place,—a bright moonlight and piercing wind." Of the next morning on the summit, he commented, "The morning twilight began as soon as the moon had set, and we arose and kindled our fire whose blaze might have been seen for thirty miles around. As the daylight increased, it was remarkable how rapidly the wind went down."

Thoreau's second visit to Wachusett occurred on October 19, 1854, when he, Harrison Blake, and the British writer Thomas Cholmondeley traveled to Westminster by train and then rode and hiked to the mountain. This time the party ascended the mountain from the south and southwest on a route that is roughly approximated by today's Stage Coach and Harrington Trails. It is this route that is described here, as it avoids the more developed side of the mountain, with its ski slopes and auto road.

WACHUSETT MOUNTAIN
ROUTE DESCRIPTION

From MA 2 take Exit 23 to MA 140 South. In 2 miles turn right on Mile Hill Road, which becomes Mountain Road as you drive south. Turn right (west) on Westminster Road. Drive about 1.5 miles west to a gated trailhead in the shadow of Little Wachusett Mountain in Princeton. There is parking here at the bend in the road by what is called Machias Pool. Please do not block the gated road. This

Administration road on Wachusett Mountain

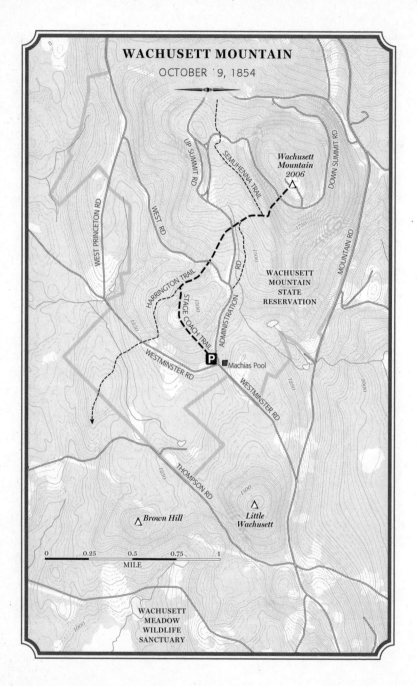

WACHUSETT MOUNTAIN

OCTOBER 19, 1854

entire hike traverses land that is part of the Wachusett Mountain State Reservation.

The Stage Coach Trail begins by ascending to the left (northwest) of the gated administration road at a trail board. It climbs northwest and north on easy grades in fields and mixed-growth forest. Off to the south lies the network of trails in the Wachusett Meadow Wildlife Sanctuary and Brown Hill. Rising steadily to the northwest, the Stage Coach Trail soon dips slightly and then intersects the Harrington Trail. At 0.5 mile bear right (northeast) on the Harrington Trail, where hardwoods dominate. This 3,000-acre state reservation boasts the largest old-growth forest in Massachusetts east of the Connecticut River. Indeed, Thoreau found a wide variety of trees and shrubs flourishing on the mountain.

Walk northeast about a quarter mile on the Harrington Trail and cross West Road, another gated park service road at an elevation of 1,400 feet. Rising steadily, the trail crosses the administration road in another quarter mile. Continuing upward in mainly deciduous woodland, it then passes a junction with the Semuhenna Trail. Keep right (northeast). The grade steepens now on occasional ledge and fragmented rock, and the trail runs through several open spots. Shortly it crosses Down Summit Road (paved) and then rises in low hardwood scrub another few hundred yards over rocky terrain to Wachusett's summit.

Thoreau found Wachusett to be an excellent outpost from which to observe a good deal of his home state. He wrote, "With a glass, you can see vessels in Boston Harbor from the summit." On October 20, 1854, he observed, "Saw the sun rise from the mountain-top. This is the time to look westward. All the villages, steeples and houses on that side were revealed; but on the east all the landscape was a misty and gilded obscurity." Looking west, he tracked the shadow of the mountain at sunrise. "Soon after sunrise I saw the pyramidal shadow of the mountain reaching quite across the state, its apex resting on the Green or Hoosac Mountains."

Thoreau and his fellow hikers had ascended Wachusett to take in the autumn color that prevailed and got a taste of colder weather in the bargain. He noted, "The country above Little Town (plowed ground) more or less sugared in snow. . . . We found a little on the mountaintop. The prevailing tree on this mountain, top and all, is apparently the red oak, which toward and on top is very low and spreading." As was his habit in these middle years of his life, Thoreau was keen to make a record of all the species he found growing here. In addition to red oak, he listed mountain ash, witch hazel, black spruce, white and yellow birch, white pine, rock maple, leverwood (hop hornbeam), beech, chestnut, shagbark (hickory), hemlock, and striped maple, all seen along the path. And from Wachusett's summit, Thoreau may have found his most satisfying view. Looking northwest, he saw "Monadnock in simple grandeur." Today a raised observation deck offers 360-degree views of central and eastern Massachusetts and the hills of southern New Hampshire. A walk around the summit perimeter will reward you with further views.

To return to your starting point, descend on the Harrington Trail from the southwest side of the summit (sign). Use care when descending over the rock and ledge, especially in wet weather. Remember to turn left (southeast) on the Stage Coach Trail. The round-trip to the summit and back is approximately 2.6 miles and can be done easily in 3 hours, though allowing for more time on top is a good idea. *Note:* There is a visitors center with a water source, food service, and toilet facilities at the base of the mountain

Harrington Trail, Wachusett summit

near the ski slopes, but no similar facilities on the summit. It may be useful to check the Wachusett Mountain State Reservation website (http://www.mass.gov/dcr/parks/central/wach.htm) to determine what services are currently available. Make sure to carry water, food, and, especially in fall, winter, and early spring, extra clothing.

7. *Wantastiquet*
(CHESTERFIELD) MOUNTAIN

The most inattentive walker can see how the
science of geology took its rise. The inland hills
& promontories betray the action of water on
their rounded sides as plainly as if the work
were completed yesterday.

—*JOURNAL*, AUGUST 19, 1851

As Thoreau enlarged the circle of his wanderings
in Massachusetts, New Hampshire, and Maine,
he also became familiar with a collection of low hills
and elevations around Concord and central Massachusetts, the raised terrain of the dunes of Cape Cod,
and the occasional new elevation come upon when
traveling. In September of 1856 he made a visit to
Brattleboro, Vermont, to see Ann and Addison Brown.
Addison Brown was a graduate of Harvard Divinity
School and had a church in Brattleboro, later becoming an educator and newspaper editor. Ann Brown

Wantastiquet State Natural Area boundary

was a botanist. Thoreau also met with shoemaker Charles Frost in Brattleboro. In Frost, Thoreau found a self-educated man who had become an adept and recognized naturalist. The two compared notes, and researchers suggest that Thoreau learned much from Frost.

On this journey Thoreau would also continue north by rail and climb Fall Mountain near Bellows Falls, Vermont, then return south to see Bronson Alcott, who had moved his family to Walpole, New Hampshire, during this period. While visiting in Brattleboro, Thoreau looked across the Connecticut River to the 1,388-foot rise known as Wantastiquet (Chesterfield) Mountain. After exploring the village, several streambanks, and a path along the Connecticut, he crossed the river one day and, with two of the older Brown children, walked uphill to see what views the summit of Wantastiquet offered.

Wantastiquet Mountain, sometimes known as Chesterfield Mountain locally, lies in the western New Hampshire border towns of Hinsdale and Chesterfield. The mountain is interesting today because of its excellent area views and new connections with a network of trails to other hills in the region. The mountain is part of a 1,000-plus-acre mix of protected land ad-

ministered by the Society for the Protection of New Hampshire
Forests, the State of New Hampshire, and the Cook Town Forest. Four adjacent summits or outlooks can be reached via a web
of paths, some of which form a section of the Wantastiquet-
Monadnock Trail.

Thoreau thought it a convenient thing to have this low
summit so close at hand. "The village of Brattleboro," he wrote,"
is peculiar for the nearness of the primitive wood and the
mountain. Within three rods of Brown's house was excellent
botanical ground on the side of a primitive wooded hillside, and
still better along the Coldwater Path. But, above all, this ever-
lasting mountain is forever lowering over the village, shortening
the day and wearing a misty cap each morning. . . . This town
will be convicted of folly if they ever permit this mountain to
be laid bare." Pleased with the locale, Thoreau went botanizing.
In his journal he listed hobblebush,
small-flowered asters, gooseberry,
scouring rush, basil, spearmint, epi-
gaea, coltsfoot, and twayblade
among the plants he discovered. As
he ranged along the streambanks
and in woods to the west, he also
found goldenrod, small-flowered
gerardia, large-leaved asters, horse-
tail, orchis, bedstraw, wild ginger,
ginseng, fleabane, speedwell, wood
sorrel, and stands of polypody ferns.
Around him were groves of maples
and patches of ground hemlock,
"with its beautiful fruit, like a red

> *"This everlast-
> ing mountain is
> forever lowering
> over the village,
> shortening the day
> and wearing a misty
> cap each morning.
> . . . This town will
> be convicted of folly
> if they ever permit
> this mountain to
> be laid bare."*

Trail on Wantastiquet Mountain

waxen cup with a purple (?) fruit in it." As always, new sections of terrain were to him fertile ground for the exploration and identification of species.

His most interesting discovery here was, undoubtedly, the hardy shrub leatherwood, which he had not seen before. "There for the first time I see growing the *Dirca palustris,* leatherwood, the largest on the low interval by the brook. I notice a bush there seven feet high. In its form it is something like a quince bush, though less spreading, its leaves broad, like entire sassafras leaves; now beginning to turn yellow. It has remarkably strong thick bark and soft white wood, which bends like lead. . . . I was much interested in this shrub, since it was the Indian's rope. Frost said that the farmers of Vermont used it to tie up their fences with. . . . This is the plant which Nature has made for this purpose."

Wantastiquet was once the site of an insane asylum and later the home of a theatrical costumer, who built a stone house on the mountain. The house ruins are still visible today. The mountain saw development where quarrying occurred, but the land attached to the house and the asylum have passed into conservation use and are now protected. Wantastiquet and adjacent Mine Mountain have an interesting history. Charles Frost, who participated in an assay of the mountain with C. T. Jackson, found the geology of the rise to include a base of argillaceous slate, mica schist, and gneiss. Fractured rock samples can be seen in different places along the trail. Frost also told the story of certain locals who, earlier, had been duped into believing there was silver in adjacent Mine Mountain and dug there fruitlessly for the rare mineral. Locals also were once convinced of a volcanic eruption here, mistaking fractured hematite for volcanic rock. Richard Wellman, writing in 1986, noted that Wantastiquet and Mine Mountains are separated by a small ravine, with the ravine walls being littered with rock and ledge. Geologists assert that Mine Mountain is of a different rock structure than Wantastiquet and is probably older geologically.

WANTASTIQUET MOUNTAIN
ROUTE DESCRIPTION

To hike Wantastiquet, take Mountain Road from its junction with NH 119 at a point just under 7 miles north and west of the point where NH 119 and 63 intersect in Hinsdale. From the west, you may cross the Connecticut River directly from Brattleboro, accessing NH 119 on the river's east side, then turning north immediately to access Mountain Road. Proceed about a quarter mile on Mountain Road to where it ends by two stone markers and a "Wantastiquet Reservation" sign. There is a parking area there. The path begins here and follows an unpaved tote road north, rising past a green-gated side road on the left. Go through an orange gate by the falling waters of an adjacent seasonal brook and continue uphill through wiry hardwoods as the path negotiates two S curves. You soon reach a second orange gate, where some outlooks to the west open up.

The trail now saws its way upward on a half dozen switchbacks, moving generally north then south on moderate grades. Soon you come to a sort of crossroads. Turn right on another path here and walk about 60 yards to the north summit of Wantastiquet, where a monument stands. Excellent views over the

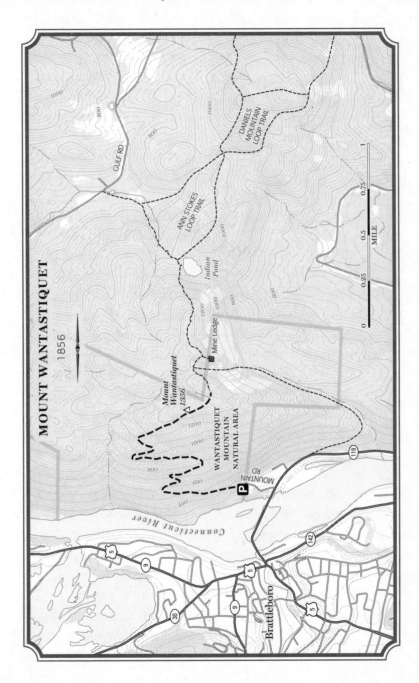

MOUNT WANTASTIQUET
1856

DANIELS MOUNTAIN LOOP TRAIL

ANN STOKES LOOP TRAIL

GULF RD.

Indian Pond

Mine Ledge

Mount Wantastiquet 1356

WANTASTIQUET MOUNTAIN NATURAL AREA

MOUNTAIN RD.

Connecticut River

Brattleboro

1000
800
1000
800
1000
1200
1000
800
640
1200
1000
800
600
400

119
142
5
9
5
5
30
9

0   0.25   0.5   0.75   1
MILE

Stone marker, Wantastiquet tote road, now summit path

Connecticut River valley are found here to the south and west, while the remaining parts of the summit ridge are wooded.

Thoreau found "the top of the mountain covered with wood," but there were open spaces, too. He had an opportunity to look into Vermont, writing, "Saw [Mount] Ascutney, between forty and fifty miles up the river, but not Monadnock on account of woods." He was able to look down at the train on which he had arrived in Brattleboro. "A very interesting sight from the top of the mountain was that of the [railroad] cars so nearly under you, apparently creeping along you could see so much of their course."

Follow the dirt road a short distance farther to Wantastiquet's south summit to gain access to the network of trails mentioned earlier. From the south summit close to the antenna array, look for the Mine Ledge Trail. It runs east to dramatic Mine Ledge and connects with the Ann Stokes Loop Trail, which affords further hiking to Indian Pond and to outlooks on East Hill. You may also access the Daniels Mountain Loop via these connectors. It is possible to enjoy a long day's hike here by following these paths to other summits and then returning. To descend, carefully retrace your steps to Mountain Road. It is 2 miles from the trailhead to Wantastiquet's open summit. The round-trip to the summit and back can be done in 2½ hours. Allow more time for exploration of Mine Ledge or adjacent elevations.

For additional maps of the area, see the USGS Brattleboro Quad; a map of the Wantastiquet Mountain Trail sometimes available at the Chesterfield Conservation Commission website (www.chesterfieldoutdoors.com/); and the Society for the Protection of New Hampshire Forests' Madame Sherri Forest map (www.forestsociety.org/ourproperties/guide/071/071_map.pdf), which covers Wantastiquet and the connected hills.

Note: Indistinct paths, side roads, and former trails crisscross the mountain at various points. Avoid these as you ascend and descend. I recommend carrying a compass and the USGS Brattleboro Quad map. Use caution if using the Mine Ledge Trail, which has a precipitous drop.

8. Mount Kineo

Thus aroused, I too brought fresh fuel to the fire, and then rambled along the sandy shore in moonlight, hoping to meet a moose come down to drink, or else a wolf. The little rill tinkled the louder, and peopled all the wilderness for me; and the glassy smoothness of the sleeping lake, laving the shores of a new world, with the dark, fantastic rocks rising here and there from its surface, made a scene not easily described. It has left such an impression on my memory as will not soon be effaced.

—*The Maine Woods*

Previous trips to Maine's North Woods had whetted Thoreau's appetite for more. On July 20, 1857, he and Edward Hoar traveled by train from Concord to Portland, Maine, then went to Bangor on the packet. They were met there by George Thatcher, who took them to Old Town, where they engaged Joseph Polis, a Penobscot elder, to be their guide. Polis agreed to a salary of $1.50 per day plus 50 cents a week for the use of his canoe. This would be Thoreau's last journey to Maine's great North Woods, an exploration of distant places beyond all settlement and a fitting sequel to his 1846 climb on Katahdin.

Thoreau and Hoar had planned a trip up Moosehead Lake, thence to the lakes near the St. John River and back south on the Penobscot. As they prepared to set out, Thoreau wrote, "my companion and I had each a large knapsack as full as it would hold, and we had two large India-rubber bags which held our provision and utensils. As for the Indian, all the baggage he had, beside his axe and gun, was a blanket, which he brought loose in his hand. However, he had laid in a store of tobacco and a new pipe for the excursion." Their possessions, including the canoe, were loaded on a stagecoach, and the three proceeded north sixty miles to Greenville, on Moosehead's southernmost shore.

Rain kept the men at a tavern in Greenville for the night, but they departed up the lake early on July 27. "About four o'-clock the next morning," Thoreau wrote, ". . . though it was quite cloudy, accompanied by the landlord to the water's edge, in the twilight, we launched our canoe from a rock on the Moosehead Lake." He described the canoe as roughly eighteen feet long, about thirty inches wide, and freshly built by Polis. He guessed it weighed about eighty pounds and thought it staunch and solid, "it being made of very thick bark and ribs." The boat, the kind that today would be called a freighter canoe, "carried about 600 pounds in all, or the weight of four men."

"It had rained more or less the four previous days, so that we thought we might count on some fair weather," Thoreau noted. "... It was inspiriting to hear the regular dip of the paddles, as if they were our fins or flippers, and to realize that we were at length fair embarked. We who had felt strangely as stage-passengers and tavern-lodgers were suddenly naturalized there and presented with the freedom of the lakes and woods."

The three men moved up the western shore of the lake to stay out the wind. Thoreau wanted to land at Kineo, about eighteen miles northwest of Greenville, and to camp there. He expected that if the wind was up, they could cross to Kineo with the wind at their backs if necessary. "The wind is the chief obstacle to crossing the lakes," he wrote, "especially in so small a canoe." Later he continued, "We stopped to breakfast on the main shore southwest of Deer Island, at a spot where *Mimulus ringens* [monkey flower] grew abundantly. We took out our bags, and the Indian made a fire under a very large bleached log, using white-pine bark from a stump, though he said that hemlock was better, and kindling with canoe birch-bark. Our table was a large piece of freshly peeled birch-bark, laid wrong-side up, and our breakfast consisted of hard bread, fried pork, and strong coffee, well-sweetened, in which we did not miss the milk."

Picking their way northward, the party had trouble finding the route through heavy mist and maneuvered carefully, staying west of Deer Island. Thoreau catalogued the birds he saw as they moved along. "The birds sang quite as in our woods,—the red-eye, red-start, veery, wood-pewee, etc., but we saw no bluebirds in all our journey, and several told me in Bangor that they had not the bluebird there. Mount Kineo, which was generally visible, though occasionally concealed by islands or the mainland in front, had a level bar of cloud concealing its summit, and all the mountain-tops about the lake were cut off at the same height."

Continuing southwesterly, the three passed the lake's westernmost outflow into the Kennebec River. The Kennebec carries Moosehead water all the way to the sea at Popham. Thoreau and Hoar were seeking a point far enough along Moosehead's shore to get roughly opposite Kineo, where they might turn east, with the wind behind them, while making a crossing. "Here we were exposed to the wind from over the whole breadth of the lake, and ran a little risk of being swamped," Thoreau noted. "While I had my eye fixed on the spot where a large fish had leaped, we took in a gallon or two of water, which filled my lap, but we soon reached the shore and took the canoe over the bar, at Sand-Bar Island, a few feet wide only, and so saved a considerable distance."

They were close to Kineo soon enough, and it was time to paddle over, whatever the breeze. "Again we crossed a broad bay opposite the mouth of Moose River, before reaching the narrow strait at Mount Kineo, made what the voyageurs call a traverse, and found the water quite rough." Thoreau wrote at some length of the danger for canoes and small boats on this enormous lake due to wind. From shore, he recognized, the lake's surface might appear relatively tranquil, but farther out even modest winds could generate waves sufficient to quickly capsize or cut a canoe in two. He also spoke of the danger of winds suddenly arising on what had been quiet waters, "so that nothing can save you, unless you can swim ashore, for it is impossible to get into a canoe again when it is upset." Moosehead is both broad and long, some forty-four miles in length at its extremes, and navigating it in a small craft can be humbling, as some find to their consternation even today. Thoreau seemed impressed with their vulnerability, writing, "Think of our little egg-shell of a canoe tossing across that great lake, a mere black speck to the eagle soaring above it!"

Polis told Thoreau and Hoar about an Indian legend holding that Kineo was a great moose that had been killed by Penobscot hunters and that the mountain had retained the shape of the moose, as if hunkered down in the lake's waters. Polis appeared to give the legend credence and asked them how they thought such a kill might have been accomplished.

> "Think of our little egg-shell of a canoe tossing across that great lake, a mere black speck to the eagle soaring above it!"

The doughty canoe came ashore at a point Thoreau described as "a mile north of the Kineo House," none the worse for wear. He estimated they had come twenty miles. "We designed to stop there that afternoon and night, and spent half an hour looking along the shore northward for a place to camp. . . . At length, half a mile further north, by going half a dozen rods into the dense spruce and fir wood on the side of the mountain, almost as dark as a cellar, we found a place sufficiently clear and level to lie down on, after cutting away a few bushes. . . . The Indian first cleared a path to it from the shore with his axe, and we then carried up all our baggage, pitched our tent, and made our bed, in order to be ready for foul weather, which then threatened us, and for the night."

Kineo is a mountain sculpted by heavy glaciation and weathering. It is shaped like a drumlin, with its highest end to the southeast. The elevation is marked by bold, abrupt cliffs on its southeast side—layers of blasted rock further roughened by glacial plucking. The mountain is formed of blue-gray felsite studded with quartz, feldspar, garnet, tuff, pumice, and a particularly valued type of rhyolite. Jackson's 1838 *Geology of Maine* called the typical deposit here hornstone. To native peoples, the mountain's rhyolite was useful in primitive toolmaking, and samples of such have been found distributed throughout New England. Bluff on its southeast side, Kineo gradually subsides in elevation to the northwest, its exposed back scraped and suppressed by an advancing mile-thick ice sheet during the Pleistocene. The cliffs on the mountain's southeast side are a dizzying 700 to 800 feet in height, and its summit provides spectacular 360-degree views over Moosehead and the surrounding country.

Thoreau, despite the unsettled weather, was eager to get to Mount Kineo's summit and to explore the local woodlands. "After dinner, we returned southward along the shore, in the canoe, on account of the difficulty of climbing over the rocks and fallen trees, and began to ascend the mountain along the edge of the precipice," he wrote. Sending their guide back to camp and telling him to come back for them with the canoe before nightfall, he and Hoar made their way upward through the still wet grass.

Thoreau observed, "The clouds breaking away a little, we had a glorious wild view, as we ascended, of the broad lake with its fluctuating surface and numerous forest-clad islands, extending beyond our sight, both north and south, and the boundless forest undulating away from its shores on every side, as densely-packed as a rye-field, and enveloping nameless

Pebble Beach under Kineo's cliffs   Maine State Museum Collections

mountains in succession; but above all, looking westward over a large island was visible a very distant part of the lake, though we did not suspect it to be Moosehead,—at first a mere broken white line seen through the tops of the island trees, like hay-caps, but spreading to a lake when we got higher. Beyond this we saw what appears to be called Bald Mountain [today Boundary Bald Mountain] on the map, some twenty-five miles distant, near the sources of the Penobscot. It was a perfect lake of the woods."

If Thoreau came here to walk the ground, others came to tour. It's interesting to compare Thoreau's account of his

Katahdin expedition in 1846 and his journey in Joe Polis's canoe and then the hike up Kineo in 1857 with the ruminations of James Russell Lowell, who arrived at Kineo in 1853. Lowell traveled to Maine roughly four years before Thoreau's expedition up Moosehead Lake and down the Penobscot River via Northeast Carry and seven years after Thoreau's extended outing in this region to climb Katahdin. Lowell edited the *Atlantic Monthly*, to which Thoreau contributed. When Lowell later removed some lines that Thoreau wrote in "Chesuncook," an article on a moose hunt that he had observed in the same region in 1853, Thoreau chastised him loudly for the omission in June of 1858: "The editor has, in this case, no more right to omit a sentiment than to insert one, or put words in my mouth." He would not publish in the *Atlantic* again until after Lowell's editorship ended, in 1861.

Lowell had come to Greenville by stagecoach from Bangor and stayed overnight there. Being a good deal more patrician in his sentiments than Thoreau, he complained of his lodgings and said of the town that it was "a little village which looks as if it had dripped down from the hills, and settled in the hollows at the foot of the lake." In his essay "Moosehead Country in 1853," Lowell complained of being overcharged when boarding the steamer *Moosehead*, which would carry him north up the vast lake. He betrayed himself as a city man, finding the great woods wanting because they were not like the metropolis. Unlike Thoreau, Lowell had come prepared to disapprove of what he found. Indeed, the temperaments of the two men could not have been more different.

As the steamer moved up the lake, Lowell softened a little. "There were three or four clearings on the western shore, but

Moosehead Lake steamboats   Maine State Museum Collections

after passing these, the lake became wholly primeval and looked to us as it did to the first adventurous Frenchman who paddled across it. . . . On all sides rose deep-blue mountains, of remarkably graceful outline and more fortunate than common in their names. . . . It was debated whether we saw Katahdin or not, (perhaps more useful as an intellectual enterprise than the assured vision would have been) and presently Mount Kineo rose abruptly before us, in shape not unlike the island of Capri." Aboard the steamship, Lowell was the quintessential Bostonian on tour, very much concerned with the surface of things, with their appearance and their similarities to foreign places. He later climbed Kineo, pronouncing it easy, and took a drink from one of its springs.

Thoreau, by contrast, enjoyed the grand outlook Kineo provided, despite the occasional drizzle. He and Hoar had what he

> *"If I wished to see a mountain or other scenery under the most favorable auspices, I would go to it in foul weather, so as to be there when it cleared up; we are then in the most suitable mood, and nature is most fresh and inspiring. There is no serenity so fair as that which is just established in a tearful eye."*

called "India-rubber" wraps and took no shelter from the wet weather. Polis, because he had no rain gear, took shelter under the overturned canoe. Thoreau wrote, "If I wished to see a mountain or other scenery under the most favorable auspices, I would go to it in foul weather, so as to be there when it cleared up; we are then in the most suitable mood, and nature is most fresh and inspiring. There is no serenity so fair as that which is just established in a tearful eye." As the two men looked down the lake, they could just make out the reflected blue tinge of a clearing sky near Greenville.

As Thoreau roamed about Kineo's summit, he found mountain cinquefoil, harebell, bearberry, Canada blueberry, wild holly, round-leaved orchis, bunchberry, woodsia ferns, and twayblade (*Liparis liliifolia*). "Having explored the wonders of the mountain, and the weather now being entirely cleared up, we commenced the descent," he noted. That evening, Thoreau woke in the night and walked about. As he did, he found several examples of decaying wood that glowed brightly in the darkness. "I saw at once that it must be phosphorescent wood, which I had so often heard of, but never chanced to see. Putting my finger on it, with a little hesitation, I found that it was a piece of dead moosewood (Acer Striatum) which the Indian had cut off in a slanting direction the evening before. Using my knife, I discovered that the light proceeded from that portion of the sapwood immediately under the bark, and thus presented a regular ring at the end, which indeed, appeared raised above the level of the wood, and when I pared off the bark and cut into the sap, it was all aglow along the log." He also found similar displays on a nearby stump. He would later write, "I was exceedingly interested by this phenomenon, and already felt paid for my journey. . . . I little thought that there was such a shining light in the darkness of the wilderness for me."

In these lines we get a sense of how such small moments, moments that might be available to us but that we ignore in the rush of modernity, were essential to Thoreau. Coming across fox fire in the shadow of Kineo meant a great deal to him, for nature did not disappoint. In such intervals, the woods offered him sustenance. "I did not regret not having seen this before, since I now saw it under circumstances so favorable," he wrote. "I was in just the frame of mind to see something wonderful, and this was a phenomenon adequate to my circumstance and expectation, and it put me on the alert to see more like it. . . . It suggested to me that there was something to be seen if one had eyes."

MOUNT KINEO
ROUTE DESCRIPTION

———⋙◉⋘———

To approach Mount Kineo from Greenville, Maine, drive northwest on ME 15 and 6 (sometimes called "the Rockwood Road") from a flashing light in Greenville center. At about 19.5 miles bear right

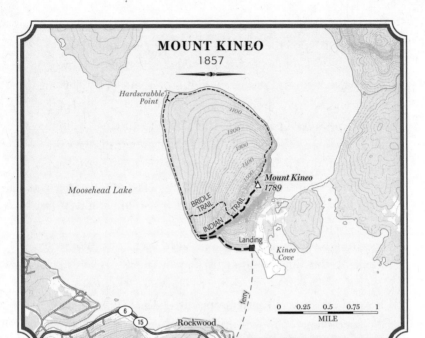

(north) on a road with a sign indicating the Rockwood town landing. There is regular ferry service from the landing that will take you across the channel on Moosehead and to the trailhead on the peninsula of which Mount Kineo is a part. Service is frequent in high summer, less so in late spring and fall. There is a charge. For information call the Kineo Shuttle, (207) 534-9012.

Kineo Township was once host to a grand hotel, begun as a tavern in 1844. Most of the structure is now gone, although the hotel's links course is still in operation. The Land for Maine's Future Program, with the involvement of the Nature Conservancy and the Maine Department of Conservation, funded the purchase of peninsula land in 1990. The Maine Bureau of Parks and Lands operates Mount Kineo State Park, which offers primitive campsites and hiking trails. There are still some private landholdings and residences on the peninsula as well.

The ferry service deposits hikers at the southwest corner of the peninsula, and trails begin from this site. From the landing point, where a trail board is located, walk northwest on an old carriage road that hugs the sandy shore. There are fine views over Moosehead Lake along the path. At 0.8 mile above the landing, the Indian Trail is on the right. This is the route Thoreau chose to ascend the mountain, one of three that directly or indirectly lead to Kineo's summit. Go right (northeast) on the Indian Trail, which rises along the mountain's southeastern precipice through stands of red pine. Grades here are moderate to steep in places, with occasional water views opening up as it ascends. About halfway up the rise, the trail passes the Bridle Trail on the left. This trail also begins at the carriage road and ascends easier grades through pretty hardwood cover. You may wish to take it on the descent. Continuing northeast and east, the Indian Trail climbs through mixed-growth forest and scrub, reaching a summit plateau bordered with conifers 0.9 mile above the carriage road. On top a former Maine Forest Service tower offers a platform for taking in the vast expanse of land and water visible in all directions from this sublime place.

From the summit, views of Little Kineo, Big Spencer, and Little Spencer Mountains lie to the northeast. Mountains around Lily Bay are seen to the southeast, and prominent Boundary Bald Mountain stands to the west. The greatest canvas is, of course, Moosehead Lake itself. Dotted with many islands, the lake's surface absorbs the marks of the rapidly changing winds and reflects the bold light of the northern Maine sky. In winter its vast whiteness is blinding. Kineo is certainly not the highest elevation in Maine's

North Country, but many have extolled the views from its summit, and it's likely you will, too. The descent from Kineo can be made by following the Indian Trail back to the carriage road, then turning left (south) along the road. Alternatively, you can follow the Indian Trail partway down, then turn right (west) on the Bridle Trail and hike down to the shore and level ground. Turn left (south) on the carriage road, following it for about 1 mile to your starting point at the ferry landing.

Note: Be sure you are aware of the shuttle schedule and have conferred with shuttle service staff as to your expected return time. Carry adequate wind and rain gear plus food and water when you hike Mount Kineo. Use caution in the area near Kineo's cliffs, and do not attempt to ascend or descend via "shortcuts."

9. Red Hill

Generally speaking, how much more conversant was the Indian with any wild animal or plant than we are, and in his language is implied all that intimacy, as much as ours is expressed in our language. How many words in his language about a moose, or birch bark, and the like! The Indian stood nearer to wild nature than we.

— *JOURNAL*, MARCH 5, 1858

Red Hill is on the short list of the lower summits Henry David Thoreau visited in New Hampshire. Uncanoonuc and Fall Mountains were worthy of exploration, but Red Hill had its special virtues. Thoreau ascended Red Hill in July of 1858 during a journey to Mount Washington with the Concord attorney Edward Hoar (see chapter 10). While the purpose of their journey was, for Thoreau, to climb Mount Washington a second time and to botanize in Tuckerman Ravine, the two broke their journey in the little hamlet of Moultonborough to take in Red Hill's splendid views of Lake Winnipesaukee and the mountains to the north. Thoreau catalogued some of the flora he discovered on the mountain and brewed tea on its summit while he and Hoar had lunch.

Thoreau doesn't say much about the terrain on his hike up this central New Hampshire rise, but he likely found the mountain more pastoral than do hikers today. Much of the hill was once cut over for pasture, and the sites of two farmsteads can still be found, their granite foundations intact. It cannot have been too long ago that Red Hill went back to woods, for young stands of hardwoods now dominate the mountain and adjacent ridges. The path follows old tote roads, which were very likely built in Thoreau's time or soon thereafter.

The walk up this 2,029-foot rise allowed Thoreau and Hoar their first comprehensive views on this trip of the nearby Sandwich and Ossipee Ranges and the higher mountains to the northwest and north. Thoreau liked what he saw, noting, "Enjoyed the famous view of Winnepiseogee and its islands southwesterly and Squam Lake on the west, but I was much attracted at this hour by the wild mountain view on the northwestward." The mountains "on the northwestward" were probably the Kinsmans or Mount Moosilauke, southwest of Franconia Notch and the Franconia Range. The men would travel through Franconia Notch on the return leg of this journey.

The two set out from Concord on July 2 with a horse and cart that Hoar had hired, and they made their way gradually north and east. On July 5 Thoreau wrote, "Continue on through Senter [sic] Harbor and ascend Red Hill in Moultonboro. On this ascent I notice the Erigeron annuus, which we have not, methinks, i.e. purple fleabane (for it is commonly purplish) .... Dr. [C. T.] Jackson says that Red Hill is so called from the uva-ursi on it turning red in the fall. On the top we boil a dipper of tea for our dinner and spend some hours, having carried up water the last half-mile."

Looking northeast from Red Hill, Thoreau noted, "Chocorua and the Sandwich Mountains a dozen miles off seemed the boundary of cultivation on that side, as indeed they are. They are, as it were, the impassable southern barrier of the mountain region, themselves lofty and bare, and filling the whole northerly horizon, with the broad vale or valley of Sandwich between you and them; and over the ridges, in one or two places, you detected a narrow, blue edging or a peak of the loftier White Mountains proper (or so called). Ossipee Mountain is on the east, near by; Chocorua (which the inhabitants pronounce She-corway or Corway), in some respects the wildest and most imposing of all the White Mountain peaks, north of northeast, bare rocks, slightly flesh-colored." He made a list of all the summits he could spy to the north, some of which he could only tentatively identify.

"When I looked at the near Ossipee Mountain (and some others), I saw first smooth pastures around the base or extending part way up, then the light green of deciduous trees (probably oak, birch, maple, etc.), looking dense and shrubby and, above all the rest, looking like permanent shadows, dark saddles of spruce or fir or both on the summits," he remarked. ". . . The landscape is spotted, like a leopard-skin, with large squarish patches of light-green and darker forests and blue lakes." Their sojourn on Red Hill completed, the two descended and resumed travel northward toward Chocorua, Thoreau observing,

"We are now near the edge of a wild and unsettled mountain region, lying northwest."

RED HILL
ROUTE DESCRIPTION

New Hampshire's Red Hill is pleasantly situated, as Thoreau wrote, in the heart of the lakes region yet perched as an outlook on the edge of an area of higher hills. To hike where Thoreau did, from the intersection of NH 25 and 25B in Center Harbor, drive northwest along Bean Road for 1.25 miles, watching for Sibley Road on the right. Turn right on Sibley Road and follow it east for just over 1 mile. Bear left on a gravel road and drive a short distance to the fire tower sign, where there is roadside parking. There is a large trail board in the upper parking lot by a metal gate.

Pass through the gate and hike northeastward through deciduous woods on a rutted gravel road in the Red Hill Conservation Area. This land is protected by the Lakes Region Conservation Trust. In a couple of hundred yards, where the ascent steepens, another road comes in on the right. The woodland here comprises mainly red oak, scattered white pine, maple, beech, and ash. The trail steepens a little and pulls around to the north and northeast. Shortly you reach a trail sign indicating the route to the tower. Turn right (east) at the sign, walking on level ground within a grove of oak and pine. The path soon widens and crosses several stone water bars and a footbridge over a seasonal brook. At 0.3 mile a road enters from the right as the trail rises. It continues over

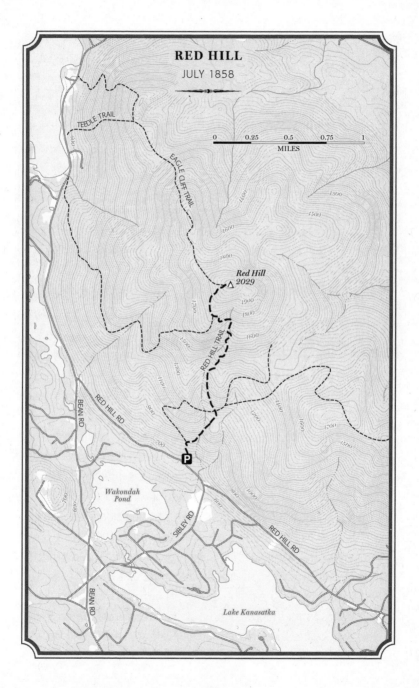

RED HILL

JULY 1858

Summit tower on Red Hill

more-level ground amid hemlock growth, with the brook to your left in a ravine. In 100 yards a tote road comes in on the left.

Next you come to the site of a farm established more than two centuries ago. Stone walls, an old cellar hole, and the foundation of a barn and corral are all that remain of the Cook family's farmstead. Watch for a reliable spring on the left side of the path and another trail board. The path bears left (north), ascending on steady grades. It continues up this rough right-of-way and winds through mostly hardwood growth on comfortable grades toward Red Hill's summit. The ravine to the left deepens, and soon the path bends to the northwest on a shelf, climbing an arm on the west side of the mountain. The trail levels somewhat and pulls

Warden's cabin, Red Hill summit

eastward again in spindly hardwood scrub. As you proceed to the fire tower, you pass the Eagle Cliff Trail on the left.

The round-trip to the summit and back is 3.5 miles and can be done in under 3 hours, but most hikers, like Thoreau and Hoar, will want to linger for a while, enjoying the outlook. Views are extensive from the old fire tower and from scattered open ledges around the summit. Views to the west include the multiple highlands of the Squam Range. To the northwest lies the Sandwich Range, as well as a number of higher mountains just south of the Pemigewasset Wilderness. Around to the northeast is the distinctive shape of Chocorua and, beyond it, limited distant views of the Moat Range. The 360-degree views from the tower are stunning,

Squam Lake and the Squam Range

with Squam Lake and its islands to the west and broad views over Lake Winnipesaukee to the southwest.

Moving about Red Hill's summit, Thoreau looked for shrubs and flowers. "On top I found *Potentilla tridentata,* out a good while, chokeberry, red lily, dwarfish red oaks, *Carex Nova-Anglia* (?), and a carex *scoparia*-like. Apparently the common *Vaccinium Pennsyl-vanicum,* and just below, in the shrubbery, the *Vaccinium Canadense* was the prevailing one. [Here's Thoreau again, as else-where, very much focused on blueberries.] Just below top, a clematis, and, as you descended, the red oak, growing large, canoe birch, some small white birch, red maple, rock maple, *Populus tremuli-formis,* diervilla (very common)." Watching for birds around the summit, he heard the chewink (a rufous-sided or eastern towhee), a bird he often discovered in his wanderings.

To head down Red Hill, retrace your steps carefully, following the trail you ascended, avoiding side roads as you descend. The Appalachian Mountain Club's "White Mountains Trail Map: Craw-ford Notch–Sandwich Range and Moosilauke-Kinsman" is worth carrying on this route. Unfortunately, it does not show the trail de-scribed here, but it does identify the dozens of other mountains in the area to the northwest, north, and northeast.

10. Mount Washington
(EAST)

———◆———

One must needs climb a hill to know what a
world he inhabits. In the midst of this Indian
summer I am perched on the top-most rock of
Nawshawtuct—a velvet wind blowing from
the south west—I seem to feel the atoms
as they strike my cheek. Hills, mountains,
steeples stand out in bold relief in the horizon.

—*Journal*, November 21, 1837

In the spring of 1858 Edward Hoar invited Thoreau
to join him for a ramble in New Hampshire's Great
White Hills, with the expectation of traveling by most
of the region's prominent summits and the intention
of climbing some of them. Hoar and Thoreau also
planned some serious cataloguing of alpine plants and
had constructed a list of some forty-six species they
hoped to find on Mount Washington. This would take
them to the mountain's striking Tuckerman Ravine,

perhaps the most interesting glacial cirque in eastern North America. They would then travel beneath the northern Presidential Range and move west to the head of Franconia Notch, where they would pursue more hiking at altitude before turning homeward. Along the way they would have many of the Northeast's higher summits in view almost constantly.

Leaving Concord with a horse and cart on July 2, Thoreau and Hoar made their way slowly northward, stopping in central New Hampshire to climb Red Hill in Center Harbor (see chapter 9), where they could take in the views of the mountains to the north and northwest. They continued northeastward, passing under the shadow of Chocorua and then along the bold Moat Range, with the lazily meandering Saco River in its foreground. Landscape painter Albert Bierstadt and other artists of what came to be called the White Mountain school immortalized these same hills. On July 6 Thoreau and Hoar camped four miles north of Jackson, in lower Pinkham Notch. Here they hired local farmer Lowell Wentworth to accompany them and act as a porter, his main task being to get Thoreau's substantial kit up Mount Washington. The next day Thoreau, Hoar, and Wentworth sent the horse back to Wentworth's farm, and the three commenced their ascent on the beginnings of a carriage road being constructed on the east side of the mountain opposite the Glen House.

The threesome hiked up the carriage road nearly four miles to what Thoreau termed a "small building a little south of the ledge." The road ended here, but Thoreau tramped upward another mile and a half on what was then the Glen Bridle Path, taking the measure of the mountain before rejoining his companions. That evening sparks from a wind-driven chimney fire in the rough cabin set some bedding on fire and threatened to set the whole building aflame before it was extinguished. From two colliers working at the cabin, Thoreau heard stories of wildcats sheltering in the cellar.

The following morning, July 8, Thoreau arose early and noted, "Though a fair day, the sun did not rise clear. I started before my companions, wishing to secure a clear view from the summit, while they accompanied the collier and his assistant, who were conducting up to the summit for the first time his goats." Thoreau paid attention to plants, shrubs, and flowers as he ascended, taking a particular interest in what he called "buck's horns," actually the gnarled and whitened roots and flattened trunks of krummholz—tangled spruce and balsam growing more or less horizontally, held down by wind.

> *"As I looked downward over the rock surface, I saw tinges of blue sky and a light as of breaking away close to the rocky ledge of the mountain far below instead of above, showing that there was the edge of the cloud. . . . There was a ring of light encircling the summit."*

He wrote, "I got up about half an hour before my party and enjoyed a good view, though it was hazy, but by the time the rest arrived a cloud invested us all, a cool driving mist. . . . As I looked downward over the rock surface, I saw tinges of blue sky and a light as of breaking away close to the rocky ledge of the mountain far below instead of above, showing that there was the edge of the cloud. . . . There was a ring of light encircling the summit." The summit that Thoreau and the others reached looked much different than the one he had reached nineteen years before. What had been a bare, wind-scoured summit in 1839 now supported two stone buildings (one called the Tip-Top House) where local entrepreneurs accommodated guests who came on horseback from the valley. Thoreau was not pleased with the change and did not linger on top for long.

He had decided that this little expedition would move next down to the lip of Tuckerman Ravine and then into the ravine itself. This required a descent of a thousand feet from Mount Washington's 6,288-foot summit over a steep boulder field of weathered rock to the southeast. The area is routinely swept by winds and clouds, reducing visibility to a few yards, and that day was no exception. Thoreau noted, "About 8:15 A.M., still in a dense fog, we started direct for Tuckerman's Ravine, I having taken the bearing of it before the fog, but Spaulding [one of the summit entrepreneurs] also went ten yards with us and pointed toward the head of the ravine."

The dense cloud cover that Thoreau termed "fog" persisted as the three men attempted to reach the plateau above the ravine headwall. Fragmented, dark, lichen-covered rock, all of it looking much alike, paves the summit cone and in cloud cover can be otherworldly and confusing to navigate. "I looked at my compass every four or five rods and then walked towards some rock in our course," Thoreau wrote, "but frequently after taking three or four steps, though the fog was no more dense, I would lose the rock I steered for. The fog was very bewildering." The three completed what Thoreau later called "an easy descent" to a point north of Bigelow Lawn and above the ravine headwall. He and Hoar looked for alpine flowers, and he found examples of *Arnica mollis* here. Oddly for an expedition centered on

Tip-Top House

finding alpine species, the route they followed to the headwall and below completely missed the richly endowed Alpine Garden, which lies just slightly to the northeast above Lion Head.

The major peaks of the Presidential Range, of which Mount Washington is the highest, support nearly eight square miles of true alpine habitat, the largest such zone in eastern North America. A unique combination of weather, temperature, soil composition, precipitation, and other factors render this space more like northern Labrador than New Hampshire. As Thoreau observed, many plant species located here are more commonly found in extreme northern latitudes.

Biology professor John Burk and research biologist Marjorie Sackett, both of Smith College, have commented on Thoreau's botanizing on the mountain: "Thoreau systematically organized his observations, setting out the characteristic plants in each zone of vegetation on Mount Washington. The first of these, three-quarters of a mile up the mountain road, was a mixed forest of conifers and hardwoods. At one and three-quarters miles, spruce was dominant with fir and birches. Fir became predominant at three miles up, the limit of well-developed trees, and from tree line to one mile's distance from the summit was a zone of shrubs or berries. Beyond that was a zone of sedge and cinquefoil and, at the very top, a zone marked by clouds and lichens. . . . As we examine Thoreau's record more than a century later, the resemblance of what he saw to what we might note ourselves in the area is striking."

Wind-bedeviled, unprotected sites on the mountain are now home to diapensia communities, bearberry, willow, and highland rush, according to Burk and Sackett. Where snow gathers, mountain cranberry, bog bilberry, and three-toothed cinquefoil are prominent. Boott Spur, the Alpine Garden, and Bigelow Lawn have large colonies of these plants. In places where snow cover is deeper and where snow lingers, mountain cranberry, bog bilberry, Labrador tea, and lowbush blueberries are common in season, forming dwarf-shrub heath communities. In areas with the most snow accumulation and the very latest melt-out, there are "snowbank communities" of dwarf blueberry, crinkled hair grass, and herbal growth. Thoreau would have seen a variety of these plants and plant groups above the headwall and in the ravine, but he would have come across many more had he deliberately hiked across the Alpine Garden.

The party gazed east over Tuckerman Ravine, named after the renowned Harvard biologist Edward Tuckerman. Thoreau observed, "From the edge of the ravine . . . we came into the sun again, much to our satisfaction, and discerned a little lake called Hermit Lake. . . . For this we steered, in order to camp by it for the sake of the protection of the wood." Descending near the north side of the ravine and climbing down about another eight hundred feet to the foot of the headwall, the men found ample snow. "We crossed a narrow portion of the snow," Thoreau remembered, "but found it unexpectedly hard and dangerous to traverse. I tore my nails in an effort to save myself from sliding down its steep surface."

Snow against the headwall lingers into summer, making the descent slippery before you get to dry rock and can climb downward with safer footing. For hikers unfamiliar with the hazards, in Thoreau's day or now, there can be surprises and the possibility of a fall. "The [snow] surface was hard, difficult to work your heels into, and a perfectly regular steep slope, steeper than an ordinary rooftop from top to bottom," Thoreau wrote.

Boott Spur and Tuckerman Ravine

At the bottom of the headwall he found the snow arch, which is usually the last snow to melt in summer. Once past this point, the three made their way eastward. "Following down the edge of the stream, the source of the Ellis River, which was quite a brook within a stone's throw of its head, we soon found it very bad walking in the scrubby fir and spruce, and therefore, when we had gone about two thirds of the way to the lake, decided to camp in the midst of the dwarf firs, clearing away a space with our hatchets," Thoreau wrote. It is actually the Cutler River that forms in the ravine, but no matter, the party had found a suitable place to rest, probably on what is today known as the Little Headwall at about 4,380 feet.

Thoreau, Hoar, and Wentworth settled down and established their camp. Thoreau noted that "the little pond by our side was perfectly clear and cool, without weeds, and the meadow by it was dry enough to sit down in." And later he wrote, "Our camp was opposite a great slide on the south," probably a reference to one of the rockfalls that dot the side of Boott Spur. "The slides . . . appeared to be a series of deep gullies side by side. . . . Some of the slides were streams of rocks, a rod or more in diameter each." The party would later walk over to Hermit Lake, which Thoreau pronounced "a cold clear lake with scarcely a plant in it, of perhaps half an acre." Two friends, Theophilus Brown and Harrison Blake, had planned to meet Thoreau on the mountain and joined him in the ravine that day.

Thoreau larked about the ravine on July 9, looking for plant specimens near the headwall. He went upward again, saying, "I ascended the stream in the afternoon and got out of the ravine at its head. . . . In most places it was scarcely practicable to get out of the ravine on either side on account of the precipices." Coming back down through the ravine, hopping from rock to rock, he badly sprained his ankle, somehow limping back to the campsite. He would be forced to sit still and recuperate for two days, passing the time chatting with Wentworth while the others climbed Boott Spur. He made notes on the clouds of blackflies that pestered them, positioning himself in the drifting smoke of the campfire to get away from the insects. Cutting down a spruce, he examined its annular rings to determine its age.

By the 12th, Thoreau's ankle was apparently recovered enough for the group to descend. They headed down to the northeast on what is now the Raymond Path, pausing to collect specimens. "It having cleared up," Thoreau wrote, "we shouldered our packs and commenced our descent, by a path about two and a half or three miles to the carriage-road, not descending a great deal." They reached the Glen House later in the day.

How much Thoreau's injury interfered with his planned botanizing on the mountain's higher elevations or in the ravine is hard to tell. He and Hoar apparently found specimens of all the species they intended to search out, and there is no comment in Thoreau's journal to indicate disappointment with this part of their expedition. Reconnected with their horse and cart, the twosome continued their travels along the north side of the northern Presidentials, crossing westward to the head of Franconia Notch and ascending the highest peak in the Franconia Range, Mount Lafayette. That effort is described in the next chapter.

MOUNT WASHINGTON (EAST)
ROUTE DESCRIPTION

As mentioned earlier, Thoreau climbed Mount Washington from the east in 1858 by walking up the newly constructed carriage road from the Glen House and then continuing up a bridle path. That he deviated from the path or explored in several directions while approaching the summit seems unlikely, given the relative speed with which he arrived on top after walking up from the road's 4-mile endpoint. You can walk the road all the way to the summit today, but given the traffic in both directions, the road may best be left to those who drive. If you are a committed hiker, you

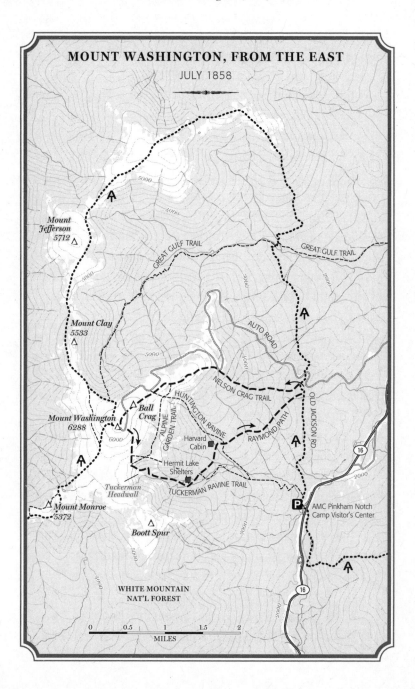

MOUNT WASHINGTON, FROM THE EAST

JULY 1858

Mount
Jefferson
5712

GREAT GULF TRAIL

GREAT GULF TRAIL

Mount Clay
5533

AUTO ROAD

NELSON CRAG TRAIL

Ball
Crag

HUNTINGTON RAVINE

ALPINE GARDEN TRAIL

Mount Washington
6288

Harvard
Cabin

RAYMOND PATH

OLD JACKSON RD

16

Hermit Lake
Shelters

Tuckerman
Headwall

TUCKERMAN RAVINE TRAIL

AMC Pinkham Notch
Camp Visitor's Center

Mount Monroe
5372

Boott Spur

WHITE MOUNTAIN
NAT'L FOREST

16

| 0 | 0.5 | 1 | 1.5 | 2 |

MILES

will probably appreciate a quieter, more wooded ascent with excellent views, one very close to Thoreau's route.

The established path that most closely approximates Thoreau's walk on the east side of Mount Washington is the Nelson Crag Trail, which leaves the Old Jackson Road about 1.75 miles north of the Appalachian Mountain Club's Pinkham Notch Camp and Visitor Center on NH 16. The Old Jackson Road is a rough, grassy former tote road that connects the Mount Washington Auto Road, Great Gulf, and northern Presidentials with Pinkham Notch Camp.

To begin this hike, from Pinkham Notch Camp walk north on the Old Jackson Road to the point where the Nelson Crag Trail departs left (west). (This point can also be reached from the auto road a short distance west of the 2-mile post and just south of where the Old Jackson Road crosses.) The trail rises southwest and west in deciduous growth, crosses a seasonal stream, and soon reaches the 3,500-foot contour line, where grades steepen considerably. Spruce and fir become the dominant conifers as the trail opens gradually to views over Pinkham Notch from Chandler Ridge at 1 mile, still rising northwest and west, but now on more comfortable grades. The path continues upward over a series of little shoulders in low scrub. Soon it ascends over more-open ledge with continuing views, passes an unreliable spring at the head of Nelson Brook, and heads west near a sharp bend in the auto road, just above the road's 5-mile post.

The trail climbs more steeply as it ascends southwest over the rocky dome of Nelson Crag and then dips westward, crossing the Alpine Garden Trail. Washington's summit looms ahead, and you are just north of the Alpine Garden, site of many unique alpine flowers and shrubs. Shortly the path crosses the Huntington Ravine Trail as it comes in from the right, then continues over 6,112-foot

Northern Presidential Range from Mount Washington

Ball Crag, with stunning true alpine views. Beyond Ball Crag the trail crosses the auto road and the tracks of the cog railway and then arrives on Washington's 6,288-foot summit.

From the summit, descend on the Tuckerman Ravine Trail, which runs south to Tuckerman Junction, north of Bigelow Lawn. This trail offers superb views over Boott Spur on the descent. (*Caution:* In wet weather the trail, which is all exposed rock, may be slippery with verglas or rime, and strong winds are common. Sneakers or running shoes are not adequate here. Cold-weather clothing and rain gear should be carried even in summer.) At the junction follow the Tuckerman Ravine Trail left (east) as it drops to the north end of the Tuckerman headwall. (*Caution:* Descend carefully here even in dry weather. Stay on the marked path.) The trail skirts the lip of the headwall, then pulls southward, dropping to the ravine floor over partially constructed rocky steps and boulders.

You may see significant snow or a smaller snow arch still lingering against the headwall in summer. *Note:* Do not attempt "shortcuts" or other departures from the trail here in the vicinity of the headwall. Injuries and deaths have occurred in this area.

The trail continues its descent to Hermit Lake and its shelters, passing Thoreau's unmarked campsite to the right as you descend the Little Headwall to the lake. Near the lake are excellent outlooks to the boulder-scarred walls of Boott Spur to the south and the steep, serrated walls of Lion Head to the north.

Continuing east on the Tuckerman Ravine Trail for a short distance, watch for the Raymond Path, which departs left (northeast) 0.3 mile below the Hermit Lake Shelters. Turn left on the Raymond Path and descend on moderate grades toward the Harvard Cabin. The trail soon crosses a stream that drops from the Ravine of Raymond Cataract and also the Cutler River. At 0.6 mile northeast of the Tuckerman Ravine Trail, this route crosses the Huntington Ravine Trail and a stream carrying runoff from Huntington Ravine. *Caution:* The trail here, which traverses a ledge at Vesper Falls, can be quite slippery in icy weather and may be dangerous when runoff is high. (See below.) Beyond the falls, the trail ascends a rise and then drops northeast on gentle grades. It crosses Nelson Brook and two seasonal brooks before pulling northward just below the 3,300-foot contour line. From this point the path descends through mainly hardwood and spruce forest on comfortable grades to a point 2.7 miles below Hermit Lake at the junction with the Old Jackson Road. Turn right (south) on the road and walk 1.5 miles back to Pinkham Notch Camp.

Note: The circuit described here is a long, challenging day hike. Fit, experienced hikers will find this loop quite doable as a 7- or 8-hour trip with time on Washington's summit. Those less experienced or unused to demanding terrain might wish to break up the trip, hiking up and then riding down on the Mount Washington Auto Road shuttle. A second day could be spent riding up the mountain on the shuttle and then descending on foot through Tuckerman Ravine and the Raymond Path as described earlier. Or, making the journey to the summit and down to the floor of Tuckerman Ravine, you might camp overnight at the Hermit Lake Shelters, then walk the Raymond Path and the Old Jackson Road back to Pinkham Notch Camp the next day. Reservations are required for the shelters and the shuttle (www.outdoors.org).

As mentioned, the Raymond Path descent, though over moderate grades and not difficult, crosses several streams, including the ledges at Vesper Falls. These are usually easy crossings, but after a heavy rain or release of snowmelt, the crossing at Vesper Falls can be dangerous, even more so in icy weather. The 29th edition of the AMC's *White Mountain Guide* suggests going around this area by leaving the Raymond Path, going uphill on the Huntington Ravine Trail for a short distance to the Huntington Ravine Fire Road, and then walking the fire road a short way south until it intersects with the Raymond Path. Once back on the Raymond Path, you can continue northeast.

When hiking the trails described here, you should always carry a compass and a copy of the AMC's "White Mountains Trail Map: Presidential Range." The more elevated sections of this hike are exposed to severe weather even in the warmer months, and a wind- and rainproof jacket, sweater, hat, gloves, food and water, and sturdy hiking boots (not sneakers or running shoes) are essential. Water, limited food service, toilets, and other services are available on Mount Washington's summit from Memorial Day to Columbus Day.

11. The Northern Presidentials and Mount Lafayette

Nature is slow but sure; she works no faster than need be; she is the tortoise that wins the race by her perseverance; she knows that seeds have many other uses than to reproduce their kind. In raising oaks and pines, she works with leisureliness and security answering to the age and strength of the trees. . . . If Nature has a pine or an oak wood to produce, she manifests no haste about it.

—*JOURNAL,* JANUARY 14, 1861

On July 13, 1858, Henry David Thoreau and his party arose from their camp by the Moose River west of Gorham, New Hampshire, in an inter-vale close to Mounts Madison and Adams. These northernmost mountains of the Presidential Range stood in the clouds, and views were limited as the men moved west to Randolph, stopping at Wood's Tavern. Rain opened slots in the clouds, and Thoreau observed, "I noticed that when it finally began to rain hard, the clouds settling down, we had our first distinct view of the mountain outline for a short time." They would contend with cloud cover all day.

As Thoreau and Edward Hoar progressed along a road that lay roughly parallel to where US 2 winds today, they had, from Jefferson onward, as majestic a view of the Northeast's highest summits as can be found. Besides Madison and Adams (with its three summits), travelers here witness the rocky shapes of Mounts Jefferson and Clay. Farther west are direct views of Mount Washington, the hub of this alpine universe, and next to it Mount Monroe, with its two separate summits. Farther west still are Mounts Franklin, Eisenhower, and Pierce (formerly Clinton), which Thoreau hiked in his first journey here in 1839.

The panorama, both bold and beautiful to those who love the high country, became visible to Thoreau and Hoar as the weather opened up during the evening they spent in Jefferson. "It cleared up at sunset," he wrote, "after two days' rain, and we had a fine view of the mountains, repaying us for our journey and wetting, Mount Washington being some thirteen miles distant southeasterly." An undercast prevailed, as Thoreau observed: "The fog clouds were rolling beneath us, and a splendid but cloudy sunset was preparing for us in the west. By going still higher up the hill, in the wet grass north of the town house, we could see the whole White Mountain Range from Madison to Lafayette."

Wherever he ventured, Thoreau seemed interested in the shape, texture, and color of mountain stone, and he commented appreciatively on what he saw from his outlook on the northern Presidentials. "The alpine, or rocky, portion of Mount Washington and its neighbors was a dark chocolate-brown, the extreme summits being dark topped or edged,—almost invariably this dark saddle on the top,—and, as the sun got lower, a very distinct brilliant and beautiful green, as of a thick mantle, was reflected from the vegetation in the ravines, as from the fold of a mantle, and on the lower parts of the mountains. They were chiefly Washington and the high northern peaks we attended to. . . . I saw a bright streak looking like snow, a narrow bright ribbon where the source of the Amonoosuc, swollen by the rain, leaped down the side of Mount Washington from the Lake of the Clouds."

Looking more to the west, he noted, "The shadows on Lafayette betrayed ridges running toward us. That brilliant green on the northern mountains was reflected but a moment or two, for the atmosphere at once became too misty. It several times disappeared and was then brought out again with wonderful brilliancy, as it were an invisible writing, or a fluid which required to be held to the sun to be brought out." As the evening took hold, he recorded, "After the sun set to us, the bare summits were of a delicate rosaceous color, passing through violet into the deep dark-blue or purple of the night which already invested their lower parts, for this night-shadow was wonderfully blue, reminding me of the blue shadows on snow. There was an afterglow in which these tints and variations were repeated. It was the grandest mountain view I ever got."

The next day, July 14, Thoreau and Hoar went to Whitefield

and Bethlehem, on to Franconia, and at last southward into Franconia Notch. Thoreau's journal records that they then began the climb up Lafayette and "camped half a mile up the side" of the mountain. They would ascend the mountain, the highest summit in the Franconia Range, by what is today referred to as the Old Bridle Path. The trail follows a long arm of the massif from the southwest, travels along the high point of this ridge, and then reaches a plateau, where the Appalachian Mountain Club's Greenleaf Hut is now found. "About a mile and a half up the path, the spruce began to be small. Saw there a silent bird, dark slate and blackish above, especially head, with a white line over the brows, then dark slate next beneath, white throat and reddish belly, black bill. A little like a nuthatch. . . . The wood was about all spruce here, twenty feet high, together with *Vaccinium Canadense,* lambkill in bloom, mountain ash, *Viburnum nudum,* rhodora."

Hikers today, like Thoreau, can witness the ravines and slides that divide or interrupt the great wall of the Franconia Range. "As I looked down into some very broad and deep ravines from this point their sides appeared to be covered chiefly with spruce, with a few bodkin points of fir here and there . . . while the narrow bottom or middle of the ravine, as far up and down as trees reached, where, of course, there was the most water, was almost exclusively hardwood, apparently birch chiefly." He and Hoar continued uphill over a series of densely wooded rock ribs to a level area, where they found water.

"At about one mile or three quarters below the summit, just above the limit of trees, we came to a little pond maybe of a quarter of an acre (with a yet smaller one near by), the source of one head of the Pemigewasset, in which grew a great many yellow lilies *(Nuphar advena)* and I think a potamogeton." He catalogued a wide variety of plants, mosses, and lichens here and noted, "In the dwarf fir thickets above and below this pond, I found the most beautiful linnaeas that I ever saw. They grew quite densely, full of rose-purple flowers,—deeper reddish purple than ours, which are pale,—perhaps nodding over the brink of a stream, altogether the fairest mountain flowers I saw, lining the side of the narrow horse-track through the fir scrub."

Thoreau and Hoar continued upward over rock and scree punctuated with tangled fir and birch thickets, seeing to the west "a line of fog over the Connecticut [River] valley." They completed the steeper climb to Lafayette's bare summit ridge soon thereafter, with Thoreau reporting, "We had fine weather on this mountain, and from the summit a good view of Mount Washington and the rest, though it was a little hazy on the horizon. It was a wild mountain and forest scene from south-southeast round eastwardly to north-northeast."

MOUNT LAFAYETTE
ROUTE DESCRIPTION

Mount Lafayette can be climbed via four different routes from I-93, which runs through Franconia Notch: the Skookumchuck Brook Trail from the northwest, the steep Greenleaf Trail from the west, the Franconia Ridge Trail (which connects Lafayette with adjacent summits, such as Mount Lincoln, Little Haystack Mountain, and Mount Liberty), or the somewhat gentler route that Thoreau chose, the Old Bridle Path. The last trail begins at the Lafayette

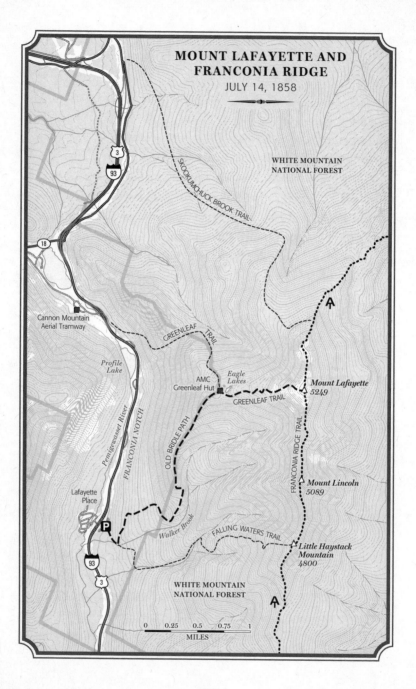

MOUNT LAFAYETTE AND
FRANCONIA RIDGE
JULY 14, 1858

Place parking areas that straddle I-93 about 2 miles south of the Cannon Mountain Aerial Tramway. You may park in either lot; there is a connecting path. Thoreau must have camped hereabouts before making his ascent of Lafayette. In his journal he commented on birds seen in this cleft between the mountains. "At the base of the mountain, over the road, heard (and saw), at the same place where I saw him the evening before, a splendid rose-breasted grosbeak singing. . . . With my glass, I distinguished him sitting quite still, high above the road at the entrance to the mountain-path in the deep woods, and singing steadily for twenty minutes."

> *"After the sun set to us, the bare summits were of a delicate rosaceous color, passing through violet into the deep dark-blue or purple of the night. It was the grandest mountain view I ever got."*

The Old Bridle Path, which runs together with the Falling Waters Trail from the lot on the east side of the highway, heads southeast through an open area and into stands of hardwoods. In less than a quarter mile the Falling Waters Trail departs right over Walker Brook. The Old Bridle Path gradually pulls away from the brook and begins to climb on easy grades.

Rising north and northeast, the trail enters the White Mountain National Forest 1 mile from the road, dips southeast again on a bluff well above the brook, and then pulls north once more, ascending steadily. There are eastward views over Walker Ravine, along with occasional views over the ravine to Franconia Ridge. This route begins in deciduous forest but soon starts to transition to balsam and spruce cover. Thoreau noted, "As we proceeded, the number of firs began to increase, and the spruce to diminish, till, at about two miles perhaps, the wood was almost pure fir about fourteen feet high; but this suddenly ceased at about half a mile further and gave place to a very dwarfish fir, and to spruce again, the latter of a very dwarfish, procumbent form, dense and flat, one to two feet high, which crept yet higher up the mountain than the fir,—over the rocks beyond the edge of the fir,—and with this spruce was mixed *Empetrum nigrum,* dense and matted on the rocks, partly dead, with berries already blackening, also Vaccinium uliginosum."

The trail brushes the lip of the ravine again shortly, going abruptly left at a set of stone risers and then right, ascending continuously. Grades increase for 200 yards, and then the path passes a short side loop with several fine views at 2.5 miles. Grades begin to relent now as the trail makes its way over several granite ribs and reaches an outlook west to the Kinsmans and Cannon Mountain. The path drops northward slightly in ruined spruce, emerging next in the open clearing at Greenleaf Hut. (For accommodations at the hut in season, visit www.outdoors.org.) Here the Old Bridle Path joins the Greenleaf Trail as the latter continues its ascent eastward over the bare, rocky upper terrain of Mount Lafayette.

Ascending the Greenleaf Trail now, you pass the two small bodies of water known as the Eagle Lakes. These diminutive glacial tarns provide a water supply to Greenleaf Hut and are environmentally sensitive. They support a variety of flourishing growth in summer. Thoreau spent time making a list of the plants he found here, which were considerable in number. His journal entry for July 15, 1858, contains a full description. Beyond, the trail rises steadily upward, dipping into rock and boulder clefts, then emerging onto the bare, open ledge and scree typical of this topmost region of

Franconia Ridge: Mount Lafayette, Mount Lincoln, and Little Haystack

Lafayette. As you meander upward, spectacular views of Kinsman Ridge and Cannon Mountain opposite open up behind you. On clear days westward views extend into Vermont.

Once on top, you, like Thoreau, can see the whole length of the Franconia Ridge Trail, which connects with Mount Lincoln, Little Haystack Mountain, Mount Liberty, and Mount Flume to the south. To the north and east lie Mount Garfield and Garfield Ridge, Galehead Mountain, and North and South Twin Mountains. The isolated landmass in the midst of the Pemigewasset Wilderness due east is 4,025-foot Owl's Head, and beyond it are the Bonds. Southeast of the Bonds are 4,420-foot Mount Hancock and 4,700-foot Mount Carrigain. Dozens of other peaks range southeast and east. Far to the east, as Thoreau commented, Mount Washington and the

Presidential Range are evident on fair-weather days. To return to the road, descend on the Greeleaf Trail and Old Bridle Path. The round-trip to Lafayette's summit and back is 8 miles and requires a minimum of 5 to 6 hours for most hikers, plus time spent on top.

As he made his way down from Lafayette's summit, Thoreau paused here and there to take note of the avian life around him. He wrote, "When half-way down the mountain, amid the spruce, we saw two pine grosbeaks, male and female, close by the path, and looked for a nest, but in vain. They were remarkably tame, and the male a brilliant red orange,—neck, head, breast beneath, and rump,—blackish wings and tail, with two white bars on wings. (Female, yellowish.) The male flew nearer inquisitively, uttering a low twitter, and perched fearlessly within four feet of us, eying and pluming himself and plucking and eating the leaves of the *Amelanchier oligocarpa* on which he sat, for several minutes."

Note: The Old Bridle Path is relatively sheltered, but the Greenleaf Trail above the hut is open to strong winds from the northwest and can be chilling or simply cold even in the warmest months. In shoulder seasons, it is colder and windier still. Hikers who attempt the mountain in winter should expect boilerplate conditions above the hut, and crampons and ice axes are often essential. Those coming up the Old Bridle Path in early spring should anticipate the need for snowshoes even if the terrain at the road is clear and dry. This trail may hold snow until quite late in the spring and can sometimes leave hikers without snowshoes postholing their way upward, an exhausting process. Once above Greenleaf Hut, hikers should carry a sweater and a wind- and rainproof jacket even in the milder months and, of course, should have appropriate hiking footwear. The route to Mount Lafayette's summit as described includes an elevation gain of about 3,600 feet.

12. *Grand Monadnock*
(SOUTHWEST)

———◦❧◦———

Many a man—when I tell him I have been on to a *mt* asks if I took a glass with me. No doubt, I could have seen further with a glass and particular objects more distinctly—could have counted more meeting-houses; but this has nothing to do with the peculiar beauty & grandeur of the view which an elevated position affords. It was not to see a few particular objects as if they were near at hand as I had been accustomed to see them, that I had ascended the *mt*—but to see an infinite variety far & near in their relation to each other thus reduced to a single picture.

—*JOURNAL*, OCTOBER 20, 1852

After several trips to Grand Monadnock over a twenty-year period, Henry David Thoreau returned to the mountain for a last, extensive exploration in August of 1860. He arrived again on the mountain as one familiar with its sprawling terrain and as one who had, over the years of his life, become a skilled naturalist. He also was, by this late date, an established surveyor who earned a modest living at his practice. It isn't surprising, then, that he created a survey map of Grand Monadnock illustrating the rangy, definitive shape of its five distinct arms. The map, one might say, captured that terrain of which he had become so fond.

A monadnock, a term probably of Indian derivation and now adopted by geologists, is an isolated hill that rises abruptly from a surrounding plain. Several mountains in New England bear this label, including Pack Monadnock and North Pack Monadnock, not far east of Grand Monadnock (see chapter 4). The distinctive massif of Grand Monadnock, with its 3,159-foot summit, lies in Dublin and Jaffrey, New Hampshire, and is climbed via paths from all directions, especially the south and east, where there is a dense trail network.

> *"Those who simply climb to the peak of Monadnock have seen but little of the mountain. I came not to look off from it, but to look at it."*

Thoreau's last journey to the great mountain saw him and his hiking friend William Ellery Channing roaming the high ground and identifying the flora and avian species found here. The pair built two primitive camps out of sight of the considerable throng who wandered up the mountain to gaze at where they had come from. Thoreau, bemused by those who came only to look away from the summit, noted, "Those who simply

Grand Monadnock's rocky top over Perkins Pond

climb to the peak of Monadnock have seen but little of the mountain. I came not to look off from it, but to look at it." This sentiment would inform his meanderings to the bogs and other interesting places of Monadnock's high plateaus during his last days of visiting here.

During this 1860 trip Thoreau and Channing climbed the mountain from the southwest and south, following a route Thoreau had used in 1858 along Fassett Brook. They then ascended more or less northward to the summit, later making camp at a site Thoreau had found comfortable on an earlier climb. After a couple of days on top, they moved to a second camp with better views to the southeast and made drier by a ledgy overhang. Most of Thoreau's camps, wherever he traveled, were simple lean-tos, both roof and bedding made of spruce boughs. This second camp abutted a wall of rock and was nearly invisible to other hikers. Thoreau and Channing stayed on the mountain from August 4 to 9.

Thoreau's hike here two years earlier had begun in Troy, where he had walked local roads to the northeast to begin his climb with Harrison Blake. In his journal for June 2, 1858, he wrote, "Almost without interruption we had the mountain in sight before us,—its sublime gray mass—that antique, brownish gray . . . that hard, enduring gray; a terrene sky-color; solidified air with a tinge of earth. . . . We left the road at a schoolhouse, and, crossing a meadow, began to ascend gently through very rocky pastures." His approach in 1860 with Channing commenced similarly.

GRAND MONADNOCK (SOUTHWEST)
ROUTE DESCRIPTION

Two contemporary routes from the south, the Royce and Old Halfway House Trails, ascend Mount Monadnock very close to the route Thoreau chose in 1858 and 1860. The rough path he and Channing followed along Fassett Brook is no longer available, and the pastures he crossed are now grown up in woodlands.

The Royce Trail, a section of the Metacomet-Monadnock Trail, leaves NH 124 roughly 5.5 miles northwest of its junction with US 202 in Jaffrey. To use the Royce Trail, you must leave your vehicle at a parking area half a mile east at the foot of the Old Halfway House Trail and walk NH 124 to the Metacomet-Monadnock

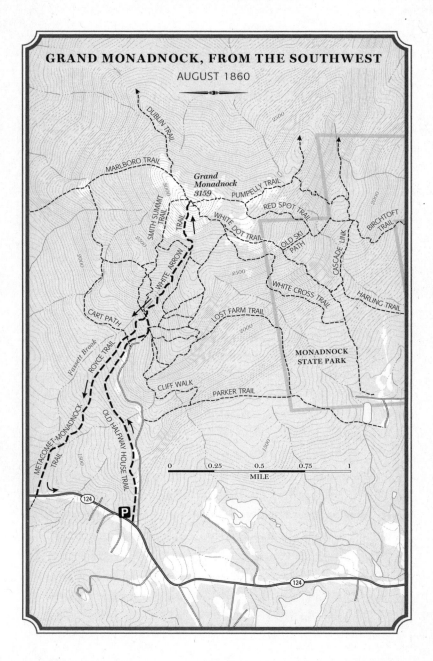

GRAND MONADNOCK, FROM THE SOUTHWEST
AUGUST 1860

DUBLIN TRAIL

MARLBORO TRAIL

Grand Monadnock 3159

PUMPELLY TRAIL

SMITH SUMMIT TRAIL

RED SPOT TRAIL

WHITE DOT TRAIL

WHITE ARROW TRAIL

OLD SKI PATH

BIRCHTOFT TRAIL

CASCADE LINK

CART PATH

WHITE CROSS TRAIL

HARLING TRAIL

Fassett Brook

ROYCE TRAIL

LOST FARM TRAIL

MONADNOCK STATE PARK

CLIFF WALK

PARKER TRAIL

METACOMET-MONADNOCK TRAIL

OLD HALFWAY HOUSE TRAIL

| 0 | 0.25 | 0.5 | 0.75 | 1 |

MILE

124

P

124

/Royce trailhead. Instead, I suggest ascending on the Old Halfway House Trail, leaving directly from the parking area, and then returning on the Royce Trail, completing the short road walk at the end of the hike. Both trails here and there touch the ground Thoreau walked along Fassett Brook.

The parking lot for the Old Halfway House Trail and Old Toll Road on NH 124 is at a gate just over 5 miles west of the junction of NH 124 and US 202 in Jaffrey. Start your hike early if you can, as this lot is favored by many who climb Monadnock from the south and parking availability may be limited, particularly on weekends. Walk left (north) on the Old Halfway House Trail along a stone wall in mixed growth west of the Old Toll Road. Follow this trail to the halfway point on the mountain's south slope. The trail rises slowly on easy grades, following the 1,700-foot contour line to the northwest on a shelf, then turns north-northeast again at 1,800 feet. Close by to the west is the Royce Trail and, a couple of hundred yards beyond it, Fassett Brook, where Thoreau and Channing hiked. When the pair hiked here in 1860, they made their way upward in the rain. Thoreau recalled, "We crossed the immense rocky and springy pasture. . . . We were wet up to our knees before reaching the woods or steep ascent where we entered the cloud. It was quite wet and dark in the woods."

The trail continues upward on more pronounced grades and at 1.3 miles above the trailhead crosses the Cart Path and passes through remnants of an old pasture. It then pulls more northeast for less than a quarter mile before coming to another trail junction. This is the Old Toll Road, which leads several hundred yards northwest to the site of the Halfway House, now long gone, its only relic an open clearing. The first structure built here was erected in the year Thoreau last climbed this mountain. He may have seen its beginnings. By 1885 a much larger mansion had been constructed, housing up to a hundred guests. The hostelry operated until 1954, when it burned to the ground. With the closing of the toll road in 1969 (though it is still used by park service personnel), much of the impact of development on the mountain's south side in the 1800s and beyond has largely faded away.

Go north on the White Arrow Trail (white blazes), which follows the Old Toll Road to a junction with the Royce, Fairy Spring, and Monte Rosa Trails, which you reach shortly. The road peters out here, and you bear right (northeast) on the White Arrow Trail, which closely approximates the route Thoreau and Channing took from this point to Grand Monadnock's summit. The path ascends more rapidly now in mixed deciduous and coniferous forest and soon crosses the Amphitheatre Trail a half mile above the junction with the Monte Rosa Trail.

Beyond the Amphitheatre Trail crossing, the White Arrow Trail ascends northwest and north and then emerges on open ledge with impressive views. The upper reaches of Fassett Brook lie just to the left of the path here in several places. The trail next rises in a steep, rocky trench leading to a junction with the Dublin and Smith Summit Trails. The three trails combine and, abruptly bearing southeast, reach the summit shortly. Except for scrub, the summit is bare rock and open, affording spectacular views. Total distance to the summit via this route is 2.4 miles.

On the afternoon of August 4, 1860, Thoreau found his old high campsite of 1858 near Monadnock's summit, commenting in his journal, "Emerged into the lighter cloud about 3 P.M., and proceeded to construct our camp." The following morning, having dried out before a campfire the night before, Thoreau arose early, later writing, "I had gone out before sunrise to gather blueberries—

fresh, dewy (because wet with yesterday's rain), almost crispy blueberries just in prime. . . . These blueberries grew and bore abundantly almost where anything else grew on the rocky part of the mountain."

On August 6 Thoreau and Channing moved their camp a short distance eastward to a more protected spot and then went to explore the lower, wet ground to the northeast. "These two swamps are about the wildest part of the mountain and most interesting to me," he wrote. The first had cotton grass in it and filled the shallow bottom of a rock basin. "The larger swamp is considerably lower and more northerly, separating the spur from the main mountain," he noted. Here he found hare's-tail, slender cotton grass, marsh willow herb, common wool grass, and turtlehead. This second boggy area, the largest of the two, is today known as Thoreau's Bog.

Thoreau also hunted berries on Monadnock's upper reaches, as he did whenever he was here. In a series of essays collected after his death and published as *Wild Fruits,* Thoreau speaks enthusiastically about the lowbush blueberries he found on Monadnock's rocky summit. "This early low blueberry, which I will call 'bluet,' adapting the name from the Canadians, is probably the prevailing kind of whortleberry in New England. . . . They love a cool atmosphere and bear in great profusion on mountains. Many years ago, when camping on Wachusett Mountain, having carried up milk for drink because there was no water there, I picked blueberries enough through the holes in the buffalo skin on which I lay in my tent to have berries and milk for supper. But they are far more abundant on Monadnock mountain. . . . On September seventh, 1852, I found an abundance between rocks on the summit—large, fresh and cooling to eat, supplying the place of water."

Despite being quite familiar with the mountain, Thoreau found the views fresh and striking as he meandered about the summit. "Each day, about an hour before sunset," he reported, "I got sight as it were accidentally, of an elysium beneath me. . . . Houses, woods, farms and lakes were seen as in [a] picture indescribably fair and expressly made to be looked at."

As he took in the broad southern and southwestern views toward Massachusetts and Vermont, he could see a cluster of mountains. "I could count in the direction of Saddleback Mountain [Mount Greylock] eight distinct ranges, revealed by the darker lines of the ridges rising above the cloud-like haze." At other moments Thoreau observed small, lenticular clouds, formed by orographic cooling, on several distant summits and just above him on Grand Monadnock. He noted, "One evening, as I was watching these small clouds forming and dissolving about the summit of our mountain, the sun just having set, I cast my eyes toward the dim bluish outline of the Green Mountains in the clear, red evening sky, and, to my delight, I detected exactly over the summit of Saddleback Mountain, some sixty miles distant, its own little cloud, shaped like a parasol and answering to that which capped our mountain, though in this case it did not rest on the mountain, but was considerably above it, and all the rest of the west horizon for forty miles was cloudless."

Thoreau and Channing broke camp on August 9 and descended from Monadnock's higher ground along Fassett Brook. Channing was anxious to get back to the comforts of home, but Thoreau was in no hurry. Whether he sensed it or not, he would not return here or to any other major mountain in his lifetime and would die less than two years later, in May 1862, still a relatively young man in his forty-fifth year.

You can descend to the road easily by simply retracing your steps down the White Arrow and Old Halfway House Trails. If you want to hike down even closer to Thoreau's route, I urge a return on the White Arrow Trail to its junction with the Royce Trail. From that junction walk southwest 0.2 mile on the Royce Trail and cross the Cart Path. There are pleasant views here and there as the trail drops quickly into deciduous woods just east of Fassett Brook and continues southwest. The grade grows less steep as you progress downward and walk through the woods where Thoreau took shelter from the rain. Pastureland clothed the mountainside nearly up to the Cart Path when Thoreau came this way, but the mountain has with time gone back to woods. About 0.3 mile above NH 124 the Metacomet-Monadnock/Royce Trail crosses and recrosses Fassett Brook and then resumes its now easy descent to the road. The brook soon pulls away, turning west and flowing into Perkins Pond.

At NH 124 turn left (east) to walk the half mile back to the parking area at the Old Halfway House trailhead where you began. The round-trip to the summit and back as described is 4.7 miles plus the return road walk of 0.5 mile. Though there are seasonal brooks along the way, Monadnock hikers should carry their own water, plus food and extra clothing. The main entrance to Monadnock State Park is on Poole Road, accessible via NH 124 about 3 miles west of the intersection with NH 137 and US 202 in Jaffrey. From NH 124 turn right on Dublin Road and then left on Poole Road to reach the headquarters. Campsites and information are available there.

Afterword and Sources

You must try a thousand themes before you find the right one, as nature makes a thousand acorns to get one oak. He is a wise man and experienced who has taken many views; to whom stones and plants and animals and a myriad objects have each suggested something, contributed something.

—*JOURNAL*, SEPTEMBER 4, 1851

Anyone who tramps around trying to find Henry David Thoreau in the high scrub of New England's mountains will, perhaps, prefer to read more about the fellow. Modern perspectives on Thoreau grow in number. Though I have chosen to become familiar with him only as hill country wanderer, anyone interested in the way Thoreau's thinking evolved over his lifetime would do well to begin with Robert D. Richardson Jr.'s masterful *Henry Thoreau: A Life of the Mind* (University of California Press, 1986). Since Thoreau is, in and of himself, a kind of archetype and, as some would say, a one-off, a sightseeker, I turned to *Sightseeking: Clues to the Landscape History of New England* by Christopher J. Lenney (University Press of New England, 2003). Like Thoreau, Lenney offers a fascinating approach to getting in touch with the disappeared New England countryside and places Thoreau in the midst of his deliberations, giving us the new term "above-ground archaeologist."

To hear what Thoreau had to say about his journey to

Katahdin, see *The Maine Woods: A Fully Annotated Edition*, edited by Jeffrey S. Cramer, curator of collections at the Thoreau Institute at Walden Woods (Yale University Press, 2009). This edition helps us find our way among the people and places Thoreau encountered on his expedition to Katahdin in 1846. Also helpful to me was *Katahdin: An Historic Journey* by John W. Neff (Appalachian Mountain Club Books, 2006). John's book will, I think, remain the best, most highly readable story of that great mountain that we will have for some time.

J. Parker Huber has done yeoman service in regularly going back to the landscape Thoreau walked, teasing out probable routes he followed and going over the ground carefully in the present. Huber's *Elevating Ourselves: Henry David Thoreau on Mountains* (Mariner Books, 1999) was very helpful to me, as was his *The Wildest Country: A Guide to Thoreau's Maine* (Appalachian Mountain Club, 1981). The Princeton Thoreau scholar William Howarth has given us *Walking with Thoreau: A Literary Guide to the Mountains of New England* (Beacon Press, 2001), which brings together extensive selections from Thoreau's writings and Howarth's commentary on Thoreau's various walks.

Among those rescued or newer works about or by Thoreau is *Wild Fruits*, edited by Bradley P. Dean (W. W. Norton, 2001). This excellent collection provides new and interesting material written by Thoreau while afield, illustrating again and again what a close and dedicated observer of nature he learned to be. A window to Thoreau's out-of-doors ideas over his lifetime are the selections in *The Journal, 1837–1861*, edited by Damion Searles (NYRB Classics, 2009). I found useful two volumes in the Mariner Books series on Thoreau, *Thoreau on Land: Na-*

ture's Canvas, edited by J. O. Valentine (2001), and *Material Faith: Henry David Thoreau on Science,* edited by Laura Dassow Walls (1999). *Nature's Panorama: Thoreau on the Seasons,* edited by Ronald A. Bosco (University of Massachusetts Press in cooperation with the Thoreau Society, 2005), offers a look at Thoreau's sentiments on outdoor exploration and observation as tied to the calendar. Included in its pages are Thoreau's remarks in July 1851, when he wrote in his journal, "The wind has fairly blown me outdoors—the elements were so lively and active—& I so sympathized with them that I could not sit while the wind went by. And I am reminded that we should especially improve the summer to live out of doors—When we may so easily it behooves us to break up this custom of sitting in the house. for it is but a custom—and I am not sure that it has the sanction of common sense." Thoreau, when abroad, often referred to the avian life he encountered as he hiked. His interest in birdlife, whether in the hills or at home, may be examined in *Thoreau on Birds,* edited by Francis H. Allen and originally published in 1910 (Beacon Press, 1993). A very important source for Thoreau's writing is the collection of the Walden Woods Project's Thoreau Institute, on which I relied often. These materials may be viewed online at www.waldenwoodsproject.org.

Maps are a useful adjunct when out hiking with Thoreau. The maps in this volume are more than adequate for hiking the routes described. Larger, more detailed maps are often helpful in placing walked ground in a larger context and in identifying other mountains and landmarks in a region. For Mount Greylock and Wachusett Mountain, see, respectively, www.mass.gov/dcr/parks/mtGreylock/ and www.mass.gov/dcr/parks/central/wach.htm. Routes on these mountains are shown on the

Appalachian Mountain Club's "Massachusetts Trail Map", as well. (All AMC maps are available at www.outdoors.org.) The New Hampshire Division of Parks and Recreation provides local maps on entry to the parks for three of Thoreau's routes described here: Pack Monadnock (Miller State Park) and Grand Monadnock East and West (Monadnock State Park). The AMC's "Southern New Hampshire Trail Map" provides excellent coverage of Grand Monadnock and the two routes described in this volume. The AMC's "Maine Mountains Trail Map" Baxter State Park–Katahdin sheet, covers Katahdin. Also for Katahdin and its region, see Maine Guide James Witherell's "The Complete Map of Mt. Katahdin and Baxter State Park." It provides a high level of detail for all routes on Katahdin and in Baxter. You can find this map in stores in Millinocket and Bangor, in bookstores, and at outfitters such as L.L.Bean and EMS. For the two hikes Thoreau completed in the Presidential Range, use the AMC's "White Mountains Trail Map: Presidential Range," which shows the entire range, north and south. For a more extensive map of Wantastiquet Mountain, see the Society for the Protection of New Hampshire Forests' Madame Sherri Forest map (www.forestsociety.org/ourproperties/guide/071 /071_map.pdf), which covers Wantastiquet and the connected hills. There are also USGS survey maps for all areas noted in this book. They may be purchased in stores or online at www .usgs.gov/pubprod/maps.html.